# Could YOU Be Autistic ?

**Stories of Self-Discovery
from Adults on the Spectrum:
How One Realizes They are Autistic**

**Anne Cossé**

*Blessed are the cracked,*
*for they shall let in the light.*

# INTRODUCTION

Ever since I was a child, I felt I was coming from another Planet.

I did not know which one. All I knew was that I did not fit on Earth, to an extent that the only explanation was that I was an extra-terrestrial.

I spent my life searching for my tribe. A group of people, a segment of society with which I could be fully myself, in all my range of atypical talents and odd weaknesses, be understood and understand others.

I tried so many avenues to find my peers: globe-trotters, political views, multi-graduates, high IQ, sexual orientation, alumni, hobbies.

Until one day I met an autistic adult.

It happened at Mensa, an association where many members happen to have autistic traits. And it all became clear. A mind-blowing evidence that explained my life, my behaviors, my thinking, my ups and downs, my professional erratic path, my social isolation, my hypersensitivity, emotional and physical. All of it.

I joined autistic groups online, researched autism so intensely I almost broke the Internet, read books, interacted online with hundreds of autistics from all walks of life, all over the world. Beyond differences in opinions, like between all humans, our minds clicked. I had found my tribe.

After a few months I felt the necessity to seek an official assessment. To be sure. To shut people's mouth when they would tell me: "You can't be autistic, look at you! Look at everything you achieved so far!"...

And after four months of weekly consultations with a professional, questionnaires, tests, interview of my parents about my childhood, more tests, she delivered a 50 page-report, and handed it out to me with those words I will never forget: "Asperger Syndrome. No question about it. Anyways I knew it the very first minute you walked in my office."

I cried of joy and relief. I mumbled: "Oh my God, I'm not crazy. I'm just autistic. Finally, at last, my quest is over..." Best moment of my life. I was 53 years old.

And then autism became my special interest, I discovered the desert in which autistic adults are left in so many countries: we get no help. Everywhere, State and Associations help is scarce, geared towards the (neurotypical) relatives of autistic (children), and when given to autistics, children are the priority.

The situation is even worse for women. For decades experts were convinced that only males could be autistic.

And for all of us, the paradigm about autism that is knitted and shared by experts and the media is wrong and detrimental.

Almost no one asks autistics any question. Neurotypicals think and debate amongst themselves about us. It is counterproductive and a source of utter frustration for us.

Meanwhile, many autistic adults are not identified. They are left to their own devices, struggling in daily life, navigating a world that feels strange and often hostile.

They struggle, and they mask, in a desperate attempt to fit in.

Masking is deeply ingrained in our behavior. Even though I am aut (openly autistic) and active in the Neurodiversity Acceptance Movement, I pondered for quite a while if I should publish this book under my real name or a under a pen name...

For the vast majority of us, finally putting a name on our difference has been an epiphany. The key to understanding and accepting ourselves, to relating to others, reaching out to our peers and not feeling alone anymore. To walking our path of self-discovery and being happier.

When an adult discovers autism and starts feeling deep inside that they might be autistic, the power of relating to other autistics and their experience is so strong that it can be lifesaving.

It sure is an element for confirmation and relief.

Hence this book.

I felt the urge to help adults on the spectrum to understand they are on the spectrum. So, I gathered the stories of autistic adults from different countries, I asked my peer friends to share their path:

How do they feel different?

How did they make the link with autism?

Did they seek official assessment and why?

Are they aut, why and what are the consequences?

What are their hobbies, job, gender identity, feelings about TV movies/series who display autistic characters?

And finally, what they specifically want to tell you.

I wish all of you who are wondering if you might be on the spectrum to find here the first answers, walk the first step towards self-understanding and self-acceptance.

On another level, I wish all neurotypical readers to understand better the autistic mind, and your deep impact on our joys and struggles.

# Vocabulary

Autism is a different hard-wiring, generating different cognition and sensitivity.

The "illness, handicap" vocabulary perpetuates the old paradigm of autism being a disorder. I never use it.

Instead, I use the following words:

- "Autistic person" instead of "person with autism"
- Assessment or identification, instead of diagnosis
- Signs instead of symptoms
- Condition instead of disorder

Yet, I have not changed the vocabulary used by the contributors in their testimony.

Common language in the autistic community, that you will encounter throughout this book, is:

NT = neurotypical = a person who is not autistic, whose neuro-cognitive system is mainstream, or typical.
Allistic = non-autistic
Autie = autistic person
Aut = openly autistic
Dx = diagnosis

# The Testimonies

When I reached out to the Autistic Community to present this book Project, the feedback went overwhelmingly enthusiastic. Many commented that they wished they had had that type of information when they were so confused about their difference and possibly being on the spectrum.

The autistic adults who contribute here have all been so genuine and wholehearted. It was not easy for them to find the mental and emotional energy to go down memory lane, to keep the focus to write pages, to talk about themselves. I am so grateful to them.

A large majority are females. It's not my choice. It happens so that few autistic males volunteered, and half of them did not plow through. It doesn't come as a surprise to me though. It reflects some of the core differences between female and male autistic traits: often times females on the spectrum share and socialize more easily than their male peers. More precisely: it is as difficult to them, but they developed better skills at doing it. Nevertheless I am grateful for those males' enthusiastic cheering up, I really am.

For every story, you will know a few personal data, here is why.

*Age.* Does autism evolve during the course of life? Is it different in young adults, mature adults and seniors?

The answer is rather obvious after reading stories of autistics from 20 to 70 years old.

*Gender.* More appropriately: what gender they identify to. Gender seems like an anodyne data. It is not. Gender atypicality and queerness is way more common amongst autistics than in the general population. The atypical way many autistics relate to gender even has a name in the Community: "the Auti- gender". All the testimonies about gender, romantic life and sexual orientation are grouped in a separate, anonymous chapter, to illustrate that point while fully protecting everyone's privacy.

*Nationality:* The contributors come from and live in different countries. Does culture impact the autistic traits or is autism a universal hard-wiring? You can make up your mind after you read all the stories.

*Self or officially assessed:* All contributors here know for sure they are autistic. Some are self-identified, and it is as good as an official assessment. Does anyone need experts to know they are on the LGBTQI+ spectrum? Same with autism. However, an official acknowledgement can be necessary, and that question is addressed in the testimonies.

I made sure they all share their views about TV series and movies that depict an autistic character (ex: *Atypical, The Good Doctor, The Big Bang Theory, Rain Man, Proof, The Big Short,* etc). Those characters are pretty much the only experience that neurotypicals get about autistics. Are they true to reality? Do real-life autistics relate to them or not?

Finally, I added a specific chapter about synesthesia. I personally see the numbers and days of the week in colors. Always the same ones since I was a child. I realized only when I discovered autism, that it was not typical. My mother asked me recently: "But why didn't you tell us about that when you were a child?", well the answer is simple: I thought everyone thought that way! Synesthesia is common amongst people on the spectrum.

I haven't altered the style nor the layout of any story, because they both reflect the thoughts process of the authors. As an autistic I instantly recognize in those texts the constant flow of thoughts and multiple connections and branching out our brains experience all the time. I recognize the impulse to go into details right in the middle of a demonstration, and then go back to the core. Or not. On, and on. It is typically autistic.

I did correct the spelling, because misspelling does not bring anything to the topic, and it hurts my eyes! I just could not leave the misspellings. Like I just can't see a wall frame that is not aligned without realigning it, no matter where I am, at some people's house, a doctor's office, my banker's lobby, wherever.

# Erin

•

38 years old
Female
Northern German, lives in Hamburg
Officially assessed

•

Ever since I can think, I have had great trouble with extreme light conditions, certain colors, certain noises/loud noises, texture and taste of food, disorganization (I started reading and writing and learning different languages at age 5 and so everything had to be alphabetized on my shelves, not just book shelves).

My parents said I was a very difficult baby and child because I had very set and rigid beliefs and routines and was unbreakable basically. But I only hid that I was easily hurt, always confused, felt inadequate, was very empathetic with others. I was hurt so much by being bullied for being different that I became very tough, rude, cold on the outside. It helped little because I still found myself with the "wrong" crowd at times. People who tried to control and manipulate me and I didn't understand it, not as a child, and oftentimes not now either.

I took things literal or understood them very differently than they were meant, I suffered from involuntary mutism, had extreme tantrums or shut down when overstimulated or I couldn't verbalize what I meant, I went through depressive spells and experienced great anxiety in social situations.

I was bullied by the other children in kindergarten and in school for being quiet, singing to myself, rocking back and forth, talking to myself, reading obsessively, writing little stories, having repetitive things, routines and compulsions I HAD to do and not being able to play with other children because they seemed chaotic and unintelligent to me.

Children and adults alike often came to me to seek advice or just unburden themselves because they said I am a good listener, but I really am not. I forget half of everything people tell me, I copy what I see on TV or what I read in books and then recycle what I hear. I do want to help people, but I'm completely lost as to how. I often do too much or too little, I can't find a healthy balance.

I was very smart as a kid but unfortunately pretty stupid when it came to real life. I forgot to put on shoes and went to school in slippers, I forgot to throw out the trash and took it to work with me later on, if I don't make lists and always control myself I forget everything. I still don't know how to pay my bills on time, take care of myself or my home. But I write awesome articles, lol. That I don't get paid for because I suck at selling myself.

I also always had "odd" hobbies. I read poetry, Poe and Nietzsche at 10ish, Shakespeare at age 13. I was obsessed with a hobby for a while or for years, then moved on to something else sometimes, only to revisit former special interests occasionally.

At age 14 I started studying religions, visiting churches, mosques, temples and synagogues or "cults" (among them Scientology and ISKCON) to take classes, speak with the followers and authority figures and try to understand why they believed what they did. After 20 years I moved on to psychology (abnormal psychology) and True Crime.

Also at age 14 I became obsessed with Heavy and Black Metal and lived that "lifestyle" (band shirts, certain clothes and accessories) until about 26 of age. I thought about working for a label and then for the medieval market that's traveling around Europe for a while too back then. I always wanted to do something that others found unusual with my life and never understood that others said I was eccentric or even that I was seeking attention. I never cared about what others do or think or how they live their lives.

I have some other side hobbies such as Barbie, Lady LovelyLocks, My Little Pony (generation 1), board games, young adult Dystopian and Fantasy literature and geekdom (geek fashion, action figures, TV shows and movies) in general that I have always been obsessed with.

Religions or Paganism aren't that much of a special interest anymore. It was replaced by psychology and True Crime. But at 14 I started out with Paganism since

I was raised Pagan, then moved on to other religions, then cultures, countries, languages, commonalities and differences.

Via psychology I got into serial killers and True Crime, then focused on three cases, Ted Bundy, Edmund Kemper and Danny Rolling. I'm currently taking a bit of a break from True Crime and don't know if I'll move away from it completely. I moved towards relationship psychology currently because of a very abusive and failed relationship two years ago.

When I get obsessed with a subject I live, eat, breathe it and dream about it even. I take my books everywhere. I work at a library so I order tons of books, I join groups or create groups, I make blogs, I write and share what I learned to give back to the community.

I work at a library because it's ideal for my special interests. Whatever I'm interested in, I can order materials for free. I hate working the front desk because it's extremely noisy in public libraries in Germany and there are screeching babies and children everywhere. It's a women-centric job, and I don't understand most of my co-workers. A lot seems to be insinuations and poison packaged as politeness. I have a friend who explains these things to me and usually I'm crushed and disappointed because I always think that people being friendly or saying friendly things means they are friendly or like me. But it's really just like kindergarten and school, just that the bullies don't beat you over the head anymore, they beat you with words.

**How and when did you make the connection between you and autism?**

I had a male friend who suggested that he was autistic, or specifically that he had Asperger's. Because I was already studying psychology (privately, for fun) I looked into Asperger's and autism in general and found a few articles about the differences between male and female autism. I read those articles and could have cried. That was all me!!! I got book after book, started looking for groups on Facebook and online and a women's group in my city and it all fit. I suddenly had all the answers to the question why I was "so weird." I am actually crying writing this because it was the moment I first didn't feel alone and misunderstood anymore.

**Did you seek an official assessment?**

I was self-diagnosed for about 3 years, I went to therapy but my therapist doesn't know anything about (female) autism, so I went to a clinic and got assessed and received the diagnosis after 2.5 months.

As a teenager, like so many female autistics, I had a general practitioner slap on me the label of BPD (Borderline Personality Disorder) although I fulfill not enough criteria at all. He saw that I was self-harming at the time and that was it. I was stuck with the label and was mistreated, received wrong medication and whenever I objected and asked to be tested for other conditions I was told I only wanted that because I was a BPD attention seeker. In my twenties suddenly doctors claimed I was Bipolar although I don't have manic episodes at all, am not promiscuous, overspend or anything else that is usually connected to the disorder. I later learned that both BPD and Bipolar are favorite diagnoses of doctors who wouldn't recognize an autistic if his ass was sewn to their faces and that my country is very backwards and uneducated when it comes to autism in general.

I wanted an official assessment because I wanted to know for sure, and to be taken seriously. I also needed the diagnosis to change my disability from BPD (which stuck, even after doctors had said for years that I don't fulfill enough criteria and the ones I do are due to completely different reasons than those with BPD have) to autism eventually.

It was difficult because my therapist, while very empathetic and helpful and friendly, didn't believe it although he had first suggested it even. I had to hospitalize myself because I couldn't handle life anymore which caused an ongoing major depressive phase. I couldn't get an assessment as an outpatient because the waiting period is over two years here.

Not having a diagnosis doctors and people didn't take me seriously. My father was always supportive of me but even he was a bit doubtful. Having a diagnosis I had the courage to talk to my employer too, take the diagnosis to my general practitioner(s) and other doctors and to alert people to some of my "odd" behaviorisms or being sensitive to certain things, explaining to them why I am experiencing some trouble right now, am agitated, am stimming or whatever else.

**Are you aut?**

I'm totally out about it. This is me. I have had people react well to it and others not so well, calling me deranged, mentally ill, dangerous, say that I was faking it because they "knew" another autistic who was non-verbal, couldn't talk or (allegedly) was "retarded" (their words), I've had people tell me that "real autism" was really the same as schizophrenia and ask me about hallucinations and if I ever killed any of my pets, or draw the connection to a US school shooter that was autistic and other things. But I don't care. Prejudiced people can go fuck themselves. I've suffered in silence for so long, I deserve to just be me without hesitation or fear.

**What are your thoughts about the autistic characters in TV series and movies?**

I think *Rain Man* was a very good depiction of one KIND of autistic, same as with the brother in *All About Mary*. But that is just the problem, for decades people thought that is what autism looks like and all of us who are verbal or have different problems, talents and so on, were ignored and disbelieved to have "the same condition."

I see myself in Sheldon and frankly, that is also why I have very few friends and only online friends. I know it's unbearable for neurotypicals to deal with my quirks. I like to write back and forth with people but hate talking to them, so no one wants to be friends with me because I want to play board games or go mini-golfing

21

and not talk at all. I find Sheldon to be realistic but again, he's only a KIND of autistic.

I never watched *Atypical* and *The Good Doctor* because I'm tired of male autistics in film and TV series. I want to see a show about a group of female autistics! And to see how colorful and different we all are. Someone with high empathy and "quirky" hobbies like astrology and another one who is very rigid, obsessed with microbiology, different ethnicities, political leanings, religions, familial bonds and jobs. Hollywood is not trying to shed light on autism or create "awareness" or acceptance but they're exploiting us. We're a trend just like vampires were in young adult literature about ten years ago. It's fine to do it with fictional people or mythological creatures rather, but we are real people, and it really hurts me personally to be represented by non-autistic actors and writers who are all about the stereotypes and who make us look like mentally challenged people.

**What would you like to say to someone wondering if they might be autistic?**
READ! Read as much as you can. Go online, look for groups online, for groups in your area, google psychologists, psychiatrists and therapists who have experience with autism, both male and female. Don't doubt yourself if you don't fulfill every single criterion, it is a SPECTRUM for a reason.

Don't go it alone, look for a trusted person or a circle of friends or family who will support you through trying to find out and whom you can toss ideas and thoughts about it back and forth with.

Assess yourself before you have someone assess you. Are you aware of all the things you do and for what reason? Keep a diary, write down things you notice about yourself, habits, routines, things that you do differently than neurotypical people. What sets you apart, what are your strengths and self-perceived weaknesses?

# Ginevra

•

54 years old
Female
Italian, lives in Italy
Almost officially assessed (it's a long story)

•

I always thought I was different, in every little thing. For example, I never played "pretend" with my friends when I was a child, neither with my younger sister when I was a teen and Mum used to tell me to play with her.

I can't do small talk, because it is a work for me, it isn't a pleasure. I get anxious when the phone rings or the doorbell rings, unless it is an appointment, and I often don't answer nor open the door.

I can do easily difficult tasks and I'm clumsy with easy ones: I need to run my "software" for everything, so it is useful for difficult tasks, and it is too slow for small things.

Currently I am a counselor, body-oriented and transgenerational, I work with groups and couples.
I am an astrologist too, and I work with individuals and couples.

My special special special interest is knowing the functioning of the human being, from brain to body, from feelings to spirit, from this life to past and future lives and other dimensions. And of course knowing myself on this perspective.

## How and when did you make the connection between you and autism?

Some years ago, I found a group on Facebook, and I was curious to read about this "Asperger Syndrome". It was a Aha-moment, so I searched tests online and I resulted on the spectrum. I was on analysis with a wonderful Jungian psychotherapist, and I asked her if I was possibly autistic, and she told me she thought I had PTSD[1], but she was ready to walk with me on the path of my self-discovery. So I went on almost 6 months studying and talking in Facebook groups with autistic people, in Italy and abroad, and then I decided to seek an official evaluation with an autism specialist.

## Did you seek an official assessment?

Yes, I did. I was 52 years old. I searched for experts in the public health service, and I found it really difficult, because in Italy bureaucracy and waiting times can be very tiring. I was trying to consult Dr. Keller in Turin.

So I thought it would have been easier to get a private diagnosis first, and then going to the public service to get the official one. I found a famous expert in Milan, and I afforded the cost of 5 private 1-hour-sessions with her, plus the train cost and the time to reach Milan from

---

[1] Post Traumatic Stress Disorder

my city. Then she said I am on the spectrum, with about a 140 IQ, and without PTSD. At that moment, instead of writing down the diagnosis, she suggested me to directly take an official diagnosis in the public health service, precisely in a public hospital in Milan, where she worked, and I agreed. "I will write down your diagnosis on public forms and you will come to the hospital in Milan twice: once to open your file and once to collect the diagnosis". I went there to open my file with a Psychiatrist, and then I … never heard of her. I tried by phone, mail, WhatsApp, Messenger, Facebook, and she doesn't answer me. I have no diagnosis, neither private nor official, I lost my money and my time...

But the Universe is now working for me: I met a Neuropsychiatrist for kids in another city, because my Association works in the health and social field, and she knows that other expert. She sometimes works with her for autistic children, and she asked her about me. She said "Yes, yes, I know, but I was busy. Be sure, I'm calling Ginevra soon". It was not true. But my friend neuropsychiatrist promised me to ask another expert about my diagnosis, Dr. Keller, who was my first choice! Now we have the COVID-19 crisis but soon I hope to see Dr. Keller and put the words THE END to my story.

**Are you aut?**
I am openly autistic only with a few people. I see that when I say it, I feel free to be myself without pretending anything. This is a bit "weird" for some people, but I am peaceful.

Sometimes I can't say it because they would not understand, and I need to work safely.

**What are your thoughts about the autistic characters in TV series and movies?**
I only watched *Rain Man*, when I didn't know anything about autism.
I can say I fear movies with autistic characters, because it is kind of embarrassing. I don't know why.

**What would you like to say to someone wondering if they might be autistic?**
Take your time to study autism and, overall, yourself. This would be a great thing in both cases, if are autistic and if you are not.

# Tina

•

36 years old
Female
Greek, lives in Greece
Officially assessed at age 36

•

I've felt different since kindergarten; I couldn't relate to other kids because my interests where different. I enjoyed playing "market" rather than with the doll house, I liked shapes and I hated group activities. In the years to follow, such differences became more apparent to me.

School years were awful because I was forced to mask in order to fit into an environment that I didn't choose. In adulthood though, masking was much easier because I had the option of environment. I chose my career (aka the working environment in which I would mask), and my friends who, contrarily to classmates are chosen.

But I have always looked for someone who thinks the same way as I do.

Besides listening to music, all my creativity goes into work. I rarely do not work. All my ideas are related to work. I simply can't help it. I want to do nothing but here comes an idea of a new website, logo, project, business plan, whatever.

I started working at the age of 20 when I dropped out of University (I was supposed to be a Kindergarten Teacher). I hated it. So, having no experience, I started as a store manager. I did some online courses and found a job as a marketing assistant and later became marketing manager.
However, I was never satisfied in companies because in all cases, after staying 2 years in the same position, it had nothing to offer; apart from a salary, there was no challenge, no new things to learn.

So I started my own business and I'm more creative than ever; I build websites, I design logos, business & marketing strategies, financial planning, etc

**How and when did you make the connection between you and autism?**
The first time I took an Asperger's test was 2012 when I was doing online research for Sleep Paralysis. At this point, I would like to make a side note: around 2008, I had volunteered to participate in a survey of the Waterloo University of Ontario, Canada about Sleep Paralysis. A few months later, I was emailed another questionnaire about ADD[2], because scientists found those two (Sleep Paralysis and ADD) relate to each other. Today I found out that, apart from ADD, Sleep Paralysis is also related to Asperger's.

---

[2] Attention Deficit Disorder

Anyway, since I didn't solve the Paralysis issue, I continued searching online and after 4 years of searching and reading, in 2012, I came across the first Asperger's test that I took. I scored high, but I didn't give that much attention back then, because I thought my answers were perfectly normal and assumed that it was a scam test where everyone who takes it is on the Spectrum. I was obviously wrong.

It took me another 8 years until I decided to take the results of the test seriously. The last 5 of those 8 years, I've been living with my boyfriend which resulted in me having no space to isolate. The lack of personal space triggered major meltdowns and fights with my boyfriend. So at some point I decided to do something about what I then believed was "anger management issue".

After a new series of online research, Feb 2020, at the age of 36, I found an amazing expert on spectrum adults, Giannis Voskopoulos, who confirmed that I'm on the spectrum and we started therapy. He has helped me understand better in what way my brain is wired, and how to turn his into an advantage.


**Did you seek an official assessment?**
With the help of Giannis, we will work on getting an official diagnosis.

I seeked diagnosis because people don't believe me. Because, if I ever have a meltdown in a public space, I must have some sort of reassurance.

**Are you aut?**
At first I told only a few friends about it. But now I say it more often. People think autism is a toddler who screams and cries; we must raise awareness.

**What are your thoughts about the autistic characters in TV series and movies?**
They're fictional characters, they do not portray reality. They're made so that the majority of the audience can relate and understand, but I wouldn't say they're a solid example.

**What would you like to say to someone wondering if they might be autistic?**
That they should consult an expert. Sometimes people are afraid to take this step because, although it is the answer to many of their questions, they are afraid they might be disappointed if the expert says otherwise. Let me tell you something though: not all psychologists can distinguish autism. If you feel you are on the spectrum, chances are you are right.

# Caitlin

•

26 years old
Female
American, lives in the USA
Self-assessed

•

I know the way I think is very different from most. It takes me a long time to accept situations or things I don't like. I look at things more logically than most people do, although they would disagree. In most situations, I feel I have an easier time separating feelings from the situation. However, there are times when I absolutely cannot, and the feelings overwhelm me. For example, any stories about harm coming to children (since having my own), I cannot think about for very long. If I do, I start to feel, which then becomes crying for a good period of time. I believe this is a prime example of how I have too much empathy, which many claim autistics do not have at all. When I was little, I used to only be able to walk over sidewalk cracks, I was very particular about my clothes, and I had major separation anxiety from my mother when going to school. My mom tried her best, but I always knew I was the difficult child and that didn't make me feel good. Now as an adult, it can be hard to avoid being depressed and angry about having been punished often and harshly for having autism (none of us knew that was the issue). Just in general I tend to think more negatively and I wish I didn't. I am highly critical of everyone and myself. I am trying to stop my natural, negative thoughts and replace them with more positive ones. I believe in always trying to be a better person, so this is one of the ways. However, it goes hand in hand with my depression; I am way more critical and negative when depressed than when I'm not. I've always been this way, it just hasn't always been expressed the same. Right now, I have two little girls, so my stress levels are consistently higher than they were previously. I also now know I have autism, so I stim freely when the kiddos are pushing my buttons.

My current job is a stay-at-home mom, because I believe the primary caregiver of children should be one of their parents. I also did not finish college, and am not good at interviewing, so it doesn't make much financial sense for me to be out in the workforce anyway. It would be nice to have some sort of a side-hustle or hobby, but that would take away emotional and mental energy from my children (since I don't have much to go around). I plan on figuring that out in the years ahead.

I'm honestly not sure if I have special interests like most autistics. I do get obsessed with things, so I suppose I have special interests that last for a short while. They're usually stories (books, movies, TV series) or games (like Candy Crush). I have a really hard time wanting to stop what I'm doing until I'm "done," which happens with several different activities, but those are the main ones. If I am interested in a TV series, I will only want to watch that series and nothing else. Once the series is over, I will get a bit depressed until I find something else to fill that time. This can be problematic with little children, so I do my best to avoid games, or watch shows that are appropriate for their ears, and I don't read as much as I'd like.

## How and when did you make the connection between you and autism?

My mom suspected I had OCD[3] as a child and later decided that didn't fit. She suspected autism as a possibility since I was middle school/high school age, but I rejected the idea. Every experience I read was about a boy with autism who was completely clueless to the world around him, and it didn't sound like me at all. Three years ago, an acquaintance posted an article on Facebook about Asperger's in girls. It sounded a lot like me! So, I spent three more hours reading many articles on autism in girls/women. I texted my mom a link to one of the articles and told her I finally figured it out. I then sunk into a depression for a few months. The articles also gave lots of symptoms of autism that I had that I hadn't even considered as being part of my problematic traits. Autism in and of itself is a communication disorder, so simply realizing I had it gave me a lot more social anxiety. I am working on getting over the social anxiety, but it's hard when you finally have a reason for why guys hardly ever dated you, employers didn't want to hire you, and it's very hard to make friends.

---

[3] Obsessive-Compulsive Disorder

**Did you seek an official assessment?**

I am not currently seeking an official evaluation. I believe I am too "high-functioning" for most doctors to take me seriously. I don't want to waste the money on something that would be a waste of time if the doctor is not taking me seriously. I am currently saving my money to get a brain-map done. I'm hoping that would officially diagnose me, as well as put me on the right anti-depressant should I need it.

**Are you aut?**

I am only openly autistic to select people: close friends, some family, and a couple doctors. I do not know if it was dishonest or not, but on some of the paperwork for my daughter's cardiologist, the question was asked if there was a family history of autism and who it was. I put yes, and it was her mother. Her doctor actually read through all the paperwork, genuinely cares about his patients and their families, and is a little awkward, so he will ask me if I am doing okay and such. For this daughter's hospital stays, it ended up on the paperwork at her first hospital when I told her nurse practitioner (despite the fact that I never gave permission for this) I had autism, since I was having a hard time coping with all the changes in my daughter's care. It made a difference for the better for the most part; the staff became a lot kinder to me. At the next hospital stay, I requested my self-diagnosis to be on the notes, and it didn't change anything unfortunately. However, it gave me the courage to walk away from a nurse who was completely overwhelming me with discharge information and let my husband take over.

My friends were surprised by the information, but accept it without question, which is nice. My mom and siblings have been accepting. It took my dad a bit to come around, but he also didn't think my daughter had Down Syndrome until her test results from a doctor came back (and you can see that on her face). We argued about it once, and he finally let it go when I said doctors would more likely diagnose me with everything else rather than autism due to the lack of research in females and the stereotypes that won't die.

**What are your thoughts about the autistic characters in TV series and movies?**

I think some of the shows show autism accurately, while many just perpetuate the stereotypes. Largely they look at what everyone thinks autism is or looks like vs. what it actually is. Generally you get a male who is very selfish and doesn't care about others. We very much care about others and are not any more selfish than anyone else. At least for me, any appearance of selfishness is simply "I am answering your question to the fullest extent about me and I am desperately searching my brain for a question to ask you back. Will you please just volunteer information about yourself?" Also "I desperately want to help you and I'm trying to figure out how to work it into my schedule tomorrow since I cannot do it today without upsetting my plans." or "The noise is literally hurting my head and I cannot hear anything else. Please turn it down so we can both enjoy each other's company." Yes these examples can appear selfish/self-absorbed, but the motives behind them are not.

Also most autistics are not savants. So... that's an annoying stereotype to keep being perpetuated.

**What would you like to say to someone wondering if they might be autistic?**
You just might be! Read as many articles as you can, watch videos, and listen to personal testimonies. Remember, it looks a little bit different for everybody! I occasionally doubt myself and have to remember how much I relate to others with autism in how we experience the world, even though we have very different personalities and backgrounds.

# Susan

•

70 years old
Female
American, lives in the U.S.
Self-assessed

•

I have been "different" most of my life. I feel it most in social interactions and sensitivity ("nerves").

Specific examples:
Socially inept.
Very sensitive to noise.
Jumpy when startled.
Inability to trust appropriately.
Treated as "different" by peers.
Odd sense of humor ~ some people might say I don't have one.

I'm retired. I worked computer jobs for 37 years. I was good at it and it paid the bills. I also had a weekend job for 7 years, clerk in a convenience store.

My current special interests are conspiracy theories and the game Magic the Gathering. I don't have any acquaintances who are interested in conspiracy theories, so I just look for interesting bits on the web. I don't play Magic the Gathering, I just collect the playing cards. I'm always interested in talking about that. So far the person I talk with the most about MTG is my grandson, who plays.

## How and when did you make the connection between you and autism?

I had a student job in a special education preschool when I was in my late teens. Some of the kids were autistic. That's when I first heard the word. All the kids in the classroom where I worked were severely disabled, by autism or some other condition.

I read a newspaper article about a high-functioning autistic man when I was in my early 20s. One thing in the article jumped out at me – the man said he had to make "rules" for social interactions because he couldn't participate without them. That absolutely described how I function socially.

## Did you seek an official assessment?

I tried to get diagnosed in my 40s. The doctor I was referred to only saw patients on Mondays. My job required me to be at work on Mondays. I decided to quit trying to get a diagnosis. I decided I was too old for it to make any difference. It made me sad, but that's about it.

## Are you aut?

I am not openly autistic. I only have a few people whom I'm close to. I got a dirty look from one of them when I tried to talk about it, and another one said "we're all on the spectrum", so I gave up.

**What are your thoughts about the autistic characters in TV series and movies?**

I don't watch much TV. I do like the autistic character, Holly, in Stephen King's detective trilogy (*Mr. Mercedes, Finders Keepers, End of Watch*).

**What would you like to say to someone wondering if they might be autistic?**

I'd say that if you need accommodations at work or at home, you should try to get a diagnosis.

# Kim

•

41 years old
Female (demigirl)
Dutch, lives in The Netherlands
Officially assessed at age 38

•

People always assumed I was shy. Though I am introverted, I am definitely not shy. I preferred to play alone, because other children made my ears hurt, acted too weird (doing wrong things like lying, stealing or teasing) and too childish for me. The local library was my refuge. I loved reading encyclopedias and non-fiction books about things like body-language, psychology and sexuality. And a lot of magazines and comic books, which was age-appropriate. I was always curious and happy to learn new info - any info. I love to learn still to this day.

I was extremely sensitive to bad vibes. My parents fought daily at the dinner table. My mother would scream at my father, cry and sometimes throw cutlery on the ground. She was very frustrated with my father's behavior, like not cleaning his own spaces, not helping her with raising the kids, not saying nice things to her or touching her. I think I got my autism from his side of the family. During fights and in other highly emotional circumstances he would laugh his head off. This would anger my mother even more. When I was 10 I asked if he was laughing at my mother and he replied that he wasn't: he was just laughing because of the bizarre situation he was thrown in: it totally bewildered him. I tested as highly alexithymic and I'm sure that he would test high as well. At the dinner table I played the good child and sometimes a mediator / translator, but then I wouldn't get listened at. The bad vibes at home and at school gave me constant headaches, stomachaches, tension in my shoulders and neck and eczema.

I was always very tired and from the age of 3 I thought about quitting life very often, which I told my mother too. She thought I was just lazy, too sensitive, looking for attention etc.

I was very clumsy. My dad laughing at me, shouting: "Typically Kim!" every time I dropped something or fell down, made it ten times worse. He was following my every move, which made me tense up even more. My mother and brother thought it was hilarious and - very eager to laugh in the house full of tension and bad vibes - they all started saying "Tyyyyyyyyyy" whenever my executive dysfunction showed its ugly head. This went on for many years. This was very traumatising for me. Thankfully, from the age of 13, when I went to grammar school, my motor skills seemed to become more fluid. Looking back I think the reason was that at my new school I was less tense, because I made some friends (my best friend being an autistic girl!!!) and I wasn't bullied there anymore.

(When I was 11 my mother told me she hated my father and that I behaved just like him. She told me that if she hadn't had me and my brother she would have left my father ages ago and then she would have been a happy woman. That she had wished to leave my father already when I was a 2-month-old baby. It was very hard for me to hear these words. They separated in 1992 and got divorced in 2008. I wished they had split much earlier, but my mother explained afterwards that she wouldn't do that because she wanted to give her children a more financially stable childhood than she had had herself in Indonesia.)

I was sensitive to the physical feel of fabrics as well: I could only wear leggings, because the fabric of jeans felt too rough for me. Of course all tags had to be cut off of clothing. And I was and still am very particular about which socks I wore (seamless for the win!).

I loved drawing, painting and crafting. I was good at it and got high grades, but I never got any compliment at home. OK, at home, when I was about 8, I drew nudes and at about 12 years old I made a very cute / childish spider family of leftover strands of wool, so the particular subjects I chose to work with may have played a role in this...

From the age of 20 I watched 330+ Japanese animation series and movies, because I couldn't spend much time in unpredictable circumstances (i.e. in the company of other people) without getting exhausted and sweaty. The genre I mostly watched was 'slice of life': ordinary things happening in high school settings with a touch of humour and romance. By the way, I studied psychology to try and learn why people were treating me horribly, but all I can assume now is that hurt people hurt people. My life after these lectures and later after workdays consisted 100% of watching these anime series.

I mainly worked in part-time administrative jobs, because I like the feeling of typing and the smell of paper. I also worked independently in stores, selling bread and cookies one year and selling organic plants and books another year. That was nice as well: using scripts in one-on-one contacts. I've been a call center-agent for a couple of years too, only doing the outbound (scripted!) calls, because I dreaded the unpredictability of incoming calls of complaining customers etc. (it was obviously a control-thing for me).
I can't work as quickly as standard people. I am much too detail-oriented. Having to work in an office garden slows me down even more because of the visual and audio distractions all of the time.
My favorite jobs have been sorting and delivering mail and cat-sitting at other people's homes. Very autism-compatible: the love of sorting stuff and cats.

As a child I loved reading in encyclopedias. Things I particularly liked reading about were biology (about furry animals like cats, the human body, sexuality), psychology (body-language and social rules) and physics (weather phenomena, space and the universe, scientific experiments etc.).
As a teenager (15?) I was really into astrology. Some years later I also became infatuated with MBTI[4] and

---

[4] Myers Briggs Type Indicator

other personality typing systems like the Enneagram. I still like these 'person sorting systems' a lot. They make humans and their behavior feel less unpredictable to me.

At the age of 20 I got infected with the anime-virus by another psychology student. I am 41 now and I still like watching Japanese films (e.g. Studio Ghibli) and series (e.g. Bakuman, Space Brothers and History's Strongest Disciple Kenichi). After watching 330+ series and movies I can now understand and speak a bit of Japanese.

I love learning and I love foreign languages. I'm doing my third modern Greek course at the moment. When I was 17 I met my first bf in Patras, Greece. We only saw each other during two vacations, but later in life I had a 'real' relationship with another Greek man in my home city in the Netherlands. At grammar school I was taught classical Greek by a handsome Dutch teacher for five years (as well as Dutch, English, German, French and Latin - by other teachers) and I've also always loved the way the Greek alphabet looks, so it was only logical to me to start learning modern Greek next. In September 2020 I hope to go on my sixth holiday to Greece, for the first time to Rhodes.
I'm very glad we live in this digital age. Google on my smartphone is like an encyclopedia on a portable mini-computer. I love learning new things and looking up stuff that peaks my interest.

**How and when did you make the connection between you and autism?**

I've always known that I was different, but reading Rudy Simone's "22 Things a Woman with Asperger's Syndrome Wants her Partner to Know" made it clear to me that I was on the spectrum. I think I read it in 2012. Nearly everything that is summed up in that book is applicable to me, which felt like a huge relief: finally I felt understood!

In 2016 my boss at that time made sure I was committed to a closed ward, because I was suicidal. They initially thought I was depressed and had some personality disorder. After just 3 days I was released. Then I got a year-long diagnostic trajectory to figure out which kind of personality disorder I had. The female psychologist I saw recognized the autism in me. On the 24th of January 2017 I got my formal Dx at the ripe age of 38.

I hadn't seeked the diagnosis because I didn't think any psychologist would believe I was suffering.
Hearing tens of thousands of times that I was a liar, a special snowflake, lazy, evil, a little professor, being clumsy and slow on purpose from both of my parents and getting hit by them made it very difficult for me to speak up about the hell I was experiencing during my childhood at home and in school. And difficult to seek an official Dx in adulthood. I also believed that the majority of psychologists still assumed autism was a male thing. So I didn't even try. And I didn't mention what I suspected in 2016.

The Dx confirmed I was a morally good person, just like I always had kept believing despite all of the abuse and bullying. It confirmed that I HAD been applying myself. I had always tried my best. The depressive and suicidal feelings I had almost always from the age of, I think, 3 dissolved. I wasn't a defective or naughty person, I appeared to be a successful autistic person!

From then on I crossed my boundaries less and less: I would go to fewer birthday parties and turned down more social outings than ever to preserve my energy. Anything to prevent myself from getting into sensory overload. I started to take care of myself better. I'm older now and have even less spoons / energy to start the day with, but I've never felt more love for myself than now (2020).

I must say that there is a lot of grief and mourning about my younger self as well. There have been feelings of frustration, anger and hopelessness I have had to work through too. Actually, in November 2019 I started EMDR[5] therapy and I am still in therapy at the end of March 2020. I can say PMT (Psychomotor Therapy) also helps me a lot.


**Are you aut?**

Yes, I am aut to most people: to colleagues at work, my family, my friends, but not to neighbors or people I take language courses with.

Why did I come aut of the closet: to prevent misunderstandings and getting bullied or ostracized again.

---

[5] Eye Movement Desensitization and Reprocessing

Why not to everyone: it takes a lot of time and energy to explain to NTs what autism is and what my own autism in particular looks like. Prejudiced people tend to shun me or start treating me as if I am mentally retarded. During brief social contact it just isn't worth it.

**What are your thoughts about the autistic characters in TV series and movies?**

I've only watched *Rain Man* and *Atypical*. I always thought Dustin Hoffman played a classical autistic man, but I read somewhere that it was not autism but another syndrome he depicted. Sadly, *Rain Man* primed most people into thinking autism was a male thing. And a very obviously deviant thing.

I watched the first series of *Atypical* and kind of liked how the boy with Asperger's was depicted. I don't have Netflix anymore now, but have heard the newer episodes are even better.

**What would you like to say to someone wondering if they might be autistic?**

Read anything and everything you can find about it online and in books. If you recognize the traits, whether it's the female presentation or the classical presentation, then I would recommend seeking a formal Dx. Like my Dx helped me get a part-time administrative job in government with two-weekly conversations with a job coach and without any deadlines (!), it could help you as well.

# Constance

•

48 years old
Hem, I think I am a human woman... but who knows !
French, lives in France
Officially assessed at age 42

•

When I remember my childhood as far back as I can, I have always been different, and the photos proved it, I was always in the background, or when my grandmother or my parents held me, I would extricate myself from their embrace, or grimace, or I gave the impression I was absent, they took pictures of me and I looked like I felt I was being attacked. My father often tried, he loved taking photos, but I didn't like it. I didn't like having my hair cut, I was crying, I was very selective with my food, well I had an unhappy childhood, parents who beat me and humiliated me, but generally, I felt that my parents were dissatisfied with me. One day, my doctor who had known me up until I was 19 told them that I was precocious with high potential, I could already read when I was 2 years old, I had started talking when I was only 1, I spoke French and Serbo-Croatian fluently, but I preferred Serbo-Croatian to French. I do not know why.
As an example, when I was little, my mother often took appetite suppressants and then would faint, she had warned me that if I ever saw her fall, I should quickly seek help from the next door neighbors. And so I was

there, watching her, barely blinking an eye, my arms behind my back, much like how a scientist observes a case. And my mother said to me "But why are you just standing there ? go and play!" I thought I was simply conscientiously fulfilling my mission, if she fell I had to go to seek help, right away, so there was no question that I must not neglect my mission by going elsewhere, especially since I would be surely too busy to see her fall if I did. So, I simply replied "I'm waiting for you to fall". Which was true. My mother became extremely angry, she was gesturing, screaming that I was a monster to want her to fall, to be dead even, etc.

Years later, I reminded her of this anecdote and she said to me "anyway you have never been close to others, you didn't care whether they were alive or dead, all that mattered was Minouche" (that was the name of our Siamese cat). Totally untrue, but that's what she believed. I explained my interpretation of the event to her, that with my diagnosis, I had been able to understand my logic years later. My mother took that as just "an excuse". I let her believe what she wanted. But between the "why can't you act like everyone else?" and "and you imitated him?" getting beaten up because I imitated my childhood friend Jojo who was a deceitful and naughty boy, who had fun getting me into trouble and have me caught... Anyway, I understood from the start that I was different from him, as well as from most others. He was playing in a way that confused me, but since most of them were playing like that, I concluded that I was the problem. In adolescence, the differences became more apparent and my suspicions were confirmed.

I did not wash very often, which made a lot of people make fun of me, my parents didn't explain anything to me, my mother grabbed me by the hair and dragged me in the shower to vigorously rub me, I had the impression that she intentionally hurt me, which must have been the case because she didn't disagree when I asked her if that was so.

There was a caring friend who taught me many things in BEP couture[6], she was like a big sister to me. She died in a car accident, her boyfriend was drunk and was able to get out of the car, but she couldn't. She was 22 years old. Since then, I had another friend who also helped me a lot and acted as a guide to know how to behave with men, accept myself, look after my house, know how to cook etc.

For a few years we lived just a few meters away from each other because there was a maid's room[7], I found a room for her because she had nowhere else to go, as there was no water at her place, and it so happened that my father had installed a private shower on the landing, I gave her the key to the shower room so that she could use it, until the day my cousin found out about it (because he was also using one of the rooms, my mother was a building keeper at the time and had access to many former maid's rooms on the 6th floor),

---

[6] BEP (Brevet d'Etudes Professionnelles) is a Professional studies certificate, Fashion trades - Clothing is a level V diploma which allows you to learn the whole process of manufacturing textile products. The holder of the diploma is able to decode the technical data of clothing design.

[7] In France, buildings from the 19th century (Haussmann) had small rooms on the last floor (6th floor) for the servants. There was a shared tap of water for all the rooms.

he reported the fact that I had given the key to my friend, so from then onwards we had to go together, secretly, so that she could wash, that's when she taught me a lot about personal hygiene.

She never passed judgment, rather she thought that I had been mistreated and that my parents had neglected me, which was not untrue, but still, she never saw me as an odd girl. I admired her, she was energetic, we played sports together, she made me want to be beautiful, to take care of myself and that's how I learned to look "human" in appearance at least. Deep down, I think that whatever happened, I was never comfortable with my appearance. I went out with my best friend's cousin and he made me feel even weirder. I was in love with him although I had a hard time understanding what love was, I was obsessed with boys, that's true, but once I had something better to do, I managed to switch it easily. Yet I remember these obsessions, I built real stories in my head, I imagined my life with them. And then when the story was finished, I think I wanted to see what other story I could make for myself.

Looking back I have always been full of imagination. As a teenager, between the hormonal upheavals and the rest, I had a very bad time through this phase, I spent a lot of time crying alone in my little room, I was afraid to talk about it because already my parents treated me like a child who just caused them problems (I still don't know what problems), so I preferred to keep my struggles to myself. One day, without knowing why, I broke down in tears in front of my mother, she hit me and said that I brought everything onto myself. As a result I was afraid to talk about it again. So, yes, if I could have read even just a little bit of Rudy Simone's 'Aspergirls'[8], I think that it would have really soothed me and maybe later on I would have sought less to experience physical sensory feelings with men, with whom I was very successful, but I felt like a strange 'thing' that had to learn more about how it functioned. You could say that I wasted a part of my life, for sure more than 30 years, maybe even 40, wondering who I was and if I was someone, or if I was just some 'thing'.

On a professional level, I was guided by my parents after the 6th grade, not because I was a bad student, I was in both a French and Yugoslavian school, but because my parents' project was to make me go back to our country, so I invested more in the Yugoslavian school than the French and as a result my grades were outstanding in their disciplines but in the French school I managed to pass with the least effort possible, just enough so I wouldn't fail and have to retake a year. That became the pretext for my parents to say that I was not intellectual and therefore put me on a vocational path. I wanted to study the fine arts, but my parents put me in the least creative branch of the subject, the clothing industry. I was told that I was "clumsy" with my hands by a teacher who persisted in harassing me and making me undo and redo the same piece over and over, when in fact I was doing the same as the others. This harassment resulted in being summoned to the career officer and the director of the

---

[8] A famous book about women with Asperger's

course, who both agreed that I behaved strangely and that it wouldn't hurt to see a psychologist at the CMPP[9]. I went there and it's true that it did me good because I saw a psychologist who told me that I didn't have to love my parents, I told her that I felt guilty for not loving them. She freed me from that pressure and guilt and after that, life was much better. But my mother noticed that I had become more rebellious, however because I had managed to succeed in a field that I hated, I preferred to stay there rather than try a new path, nothing else that was offered pleased me anyway, so I finished my CAP[10], I obtained it against all expectations, based on grades, In the last year, the teacher liked me very much and my grades were excellent, I achieved my CAP, then my BEP after, however during the first year of my BEP I had a teacher who was relentless towards me until I eventually had a full-blown crisis. This time, I stormed out and threatened to file a complaint. She caught up with me and calmed herself down, she decided to entrust me with the organization aspect of the Bicentenary parade because I did not want to be the silly one presenting the models. I organized it superbly and I was praised for it.

After a while, I wanted to resume my studies, but because I did not yet have the appropriate level, my

---

[9] The CMPP (medico-psycho-educational center) is a place of listening, prevention and care, is aimed at children and adolescents up to the age of 20 who are experiencing learning difficulties, psychomotor, language or behavioral disorders, with family or at school.
[10] The certificate of professional aptitude (C.A.P.) gives a qualification of worker or qualified employee in a given trade. There are approximately 200 specialties of C.A.P.

father paid for two years of private school, but I had passed from a BEP level to a general education program. Suffice to say that I had 10 years to catch up to the right level for the baccalaureate, yet I caught up with it well. I did not complete it because at that stage I realized I had success with boys (between about 17 and 19 years old, I realized that I wanted to see what it was like to go out with real "Kens", I had played with Barbie dolls until I was 15, but I also played toy cars and construction games). So afterwards I left school and worked as a secretary, then having learned a certain rigor from lawyers, I resumed studying law, then stopped, I wanted to study psychology but my parents did not want to further invest in me, and I did not have the means to continue. By 25 years old, I had done a lot of little things, I held a BAFA[11], a DAEU[12], I did a lot of different things and worked in various fields. I think I managed to learn a lot from both my experiences as well as from TV series and movies that I watched over and over again, as soon as I had a VHS player and then a DVD player, I was able to record shows, series, movies, and even books, because I have always loved reading. In fact everything that I came across that inspired me I reused to make it part of my laboratory of social skills. It's this ability to retain thousands of phrases and discussions that enabled me

---

[11] The Brevet d'Aptitude aux Fonctions d'Animateur (BAFA), is a certificate that enables a person to be a youth activity leader.
[12] In France, a Diplôme d'Accès aux Etudes Universitaires (DAEU) is a degree from a French university in order to have an equivalence of the Baccalauréat and access to university studies.

to be what I wanted to be, so I managed to get hired through mimicry that matched expectations.

In hindsight I have always struggled with punctuality. It's impossible for me to estimate time or quantities, I thought I would never have my driver's license, but I finally got it at 45 years old. So since March 14 of this year, I'm no longer a 'learner driver'. Yeah! However I passed it this time in an automatic car, I didn't want the gearbox to distract me, I managed to use it for high gears but I had trouble figuring out how to use the gears in reverse, like going from high to low gears, it was stressing me out at high speed. But now, with the automatic transmission, I have no problem. I am even a good driver, my companion says that I drive so well that he wants to follow my example when he passes his license. So, even though he is the first to make jokes about women behind the wheel, he boasts of having a woman who drives like a soldier. It's funny. Because that's how I see myself, sometimes, a soldier who has fought battles and participated in many wars.

I became a mother at the age of 25, I had always said that I wanted to be a mother at 25, I do not know why, I like this figure, it was for me a sufficiently mature age but not too old... I met the father of my daughter following a depression after losing a lover at the time. I couldn't love my daughter's father, I think he was autistic too, but we could never talk about this hypothesis because his parents refused to consider this as a possibility. But for me it's clear that he was. We separated when our daughter was 2 years old, he spent his time on the games console and no longer worked,

58

he was so self-absorbed that I had a hard time living with him. I fought for my daughter and in time, she was the one who revealed me to myself. I owe her a lot. Hence my investment too, in part. I became a full-time mother, taking care of my daughter but also having lots of projects, I wrote a book, well two complete and two or three unfinished. I have also campaigned a lot in the autism community.

## What are your hobbies?

My very first hobby was Barbie dolls. Then when my parents forced me to learn dressmaking I made them dresses. I hated it, but it got me my first job when I was 16, in a ready-to-wear shop while on vacation. Also drawing has been an interest for a long time. I always read the same books (I only had a few, but my mother gave me her Harlequins[13], the Blue Grass, Sophie's Misfortunes, I compared my mother to the Countess of Fichini, I also read the biography of Hellen Keller)... and would read all these over and over again.

TV series have allowed me to access my specific interest for many years, observing behavior. I also had an organic period when I learned to cook, make bread, yogurts, everything, in fact. Nothing learned is useless. Still now, I am very interested in essential oils and natural remedies. Autism has been of specific interest, but in fact all the disorders and diseases. Neuroscience especially. But recently, I admit, cars (since I discovered

---

[13] Harlequin is a publishing company specializing in easy-reading romance novels

I needed to learn about it myself so I wouldn't be taken advantage of by the seller or by the mechanic)... I am told that I learn things thoroughly... I don't see what good it would be to just be 'a DIY cowboy'?!

That said I also like creating art, writing, I have an ease in writing (I don't like to talk too much, it quickly wears me out), I'd rather communicate through the keyboard. Otherwise, I like to mosaic, I like to do DIY, the concept of the D system[14] has been vital for me. My dad once told me it was better if I could avoid paying someone to do something that I could do for myself. So I took that to heart and generalized it to all aspects of my life. At the moment, I've returned to sewing. I like to make bags, I started making patterns during this time of confinement[15]. I really want to get back into it more actively.

The behavior of people has really disgusted me lately, I really want to isolate myself somewhere and do what I love with my hands and leave my head a little. Maybe the rest will come back to me. But after a depression following a bad encounter with my ex-boyfriend, who was 18 years younger than me, and his family of psychopaths, I realized that in general humans and I do not have much affinity. Well, yes I do have friends, people that I really appreciate and others that I love, I

---

[14] "Système D", the letter D refers to any one of the French nouns 'débrouille', 'débrouillardise' or 'démerde' (French slang). The verbs *se débrouiller* and *se démerder* mean to make do, to manage, especially in an adverse situation. Basically, it refers to one's ability and need to be resourceful.
[15] This has been written during the national lockdown and quarantine due to Covid-19

have been living as part of a couple for the past 2 years (it's a blended family, he has a son and a rabbit and I have a daughter and two cats).

As a result, I think that the creativity that I have had for a while allows me to return to things that I used to do that give me a lot of pleasure and relaxation. I'm learning to relax without having to take a multitude of soothing essential oils (phyto treatments). My companion also shares my desire to create an artistic / craft activity, which helps me stay centered.

**What is your current job? Why?**
I told  the MDPH in Haute-Garonne informally, so that they understood that I was fighting for my daughter, not for the money, otherwise I would have requested a disability allowance for myself as well, and they understood that I only had good intentions, so, I got enough support for my daughter, and I'm able to be her official career. Which also keeps me from others in a way. I receive a salary via CESU[16]  and I do not have to depend on anyone.
For the moment, I take care of my daughter full time, but gradually we will create a somewhat 'family' business, so my daughter can train and have a job that allows her to find her own way, but she too is an artist at heart. This is in development.

─────────────────────────

[16] Le Chèque Emploi Service Universel (CESU) = universal service employment check. It is a payment voucher, it's main objective is to pay for the provision of personal services at home and childcare outside the home. It also allows you to pay the bill of a personal service provider.

**How and when did you make the connection between you and autism?**

I did not make the connection on my own. In fact, I thought I had ADHD[17] as I was hyperactive at the beginning, but very quickly, the president of the association told me no I am not, even though a psychiatrist who wanted to get me into his (new) ADHD categories thought so, but actually, looking back I think he asked the questions wrong. In fact, I tried methylphenidate and antidepressants and they did not have the desired effect. It actually seemed to increase my autistic symptoms even more. Obsession to the point of praising a pencil, a women's journal, etc. When I stopped I realized that "the truth is out there" (as the TV series says).

So, when my daughter was diagnosed at the age of 8, I participated in autism discussion groups and all that, but I was always ejected from the groups. I was always blamed for things that I did not understand. One day I came across a woman who claimed to have autism with Asperger's syndrome and she told me that I was also probably autistic with Asperger's syndrome. I laughed a lot as a response, but actually I had met women with Asperger's and I realized that I had enough doubts to start asking myself questions about my own traits. But I was warned, 'be careful' that I wouldn't be able to get a diagnosis 'just like that' etc etc. Around this time I came across a sort of 'autistic' predator (I doubt he was actually autistic in fact) who told me that I would never be able to get a diagnosis from the CHU in Créteil,

---

[17] Attention deficit hyperactivity disorder

therefore, (maybe in the spirit of defiance?) I wrote to the Service of Professor Marion Leboyer, whom I met personally and then shortly after, I was summoned and given the diagnosis following days of observation with her team. But it was a lecture by Tony Attwood's that had been sent to me by an Aspie friend which was a real revelation to me. I cried for days! When I went back to see the psychiatrist who diagnosed me with ADHD, he reluctantly admitted his mistake and that now, in fact, it was more likely that I was autistic.

In fact, I followed a path that allowed me to have positive encounters. After which, I either followed the person's advice to do or not do something... I understood over time that this is what I had been missing, but I did not want to get a diagnosis to have any rights one way or the other, besides I did not take steps for myself at the MDPH , I just spoke to them to explain that it was not to have money to which I was not entitled, but that my daughter's life had been ruined because they had put sticks in my wheels for support through the private sector.

But it is clear that if I had been diagnosed earlier, maybe I would not have had the same life of suffering, or maybe it would have been worse. My father told me to put my daughter in an institution and start my life over, so I cut ties with him. I think that in my situation, it would surely have gone against me, but if at least I had known it ...just for myself... how many mistakes and how much time wasted wondering about why I was different could have been avoided? It's been 6 years since I received my diagnosis and I keep on going up and down in the emotions towards this condition, sometimes rejection, sometimes acceptance, sometimes a step backwards, sometimes .... nothing, withdraw but able to socialize for short periods.

**Are you aut?**

I spoke about it at the beginning to my mother who immediately refused the diagnosis, she was in denial. Then she moderately accepted it, but sprinkled conversation with crushing little sentences, like 'don't make yourself more autistic than you are' or things like that, 'you make your autism too much', 'you weren't like that before' ... but she ended up not talking about it with me anymore, maybe she accepted it or maybe she made it a taboo subject... especially since she had introduced this taboo thing with my father already, she made him out to be a sort of tyrant, a spoiled child. My father has always been narcissistic, but he could have good sides, whereas my mother, she is a borderline narcissist I would say. If she has autism, she hides it well. But I get my autism from my paternal grandmother. She died at 98 years old. She was a wonderful woman. She could neither read nor write, but she knew her bible by heart. You could not change the punctuation or a word in any of the passages, she knew and she corrected you. And she had this 'bad people scanner', she felt people. I have the same. I think that when we have no choice we use our 6th sense to detect good or bad souls.

Otherwise I'm open about it on Facebook but always on condition of anonymity, and I avoid giving out my real name. With shopkeepers, it happened I talked about it but I don't routinely mention it, nor to people who are not already interested in it. If the conversation is going well, and if for example, it's in relation to my daughter, then we might broach the subject and I'm able to speak about it, but rarely. Colleagues I don't have any. I've shared with people who are close to me, like my friends, the others I have not spoken about it, once I mentioned it to my cousin's wife and she started spouting so much nonsense to me that I was probably 'schizo' like my father (who is not schizo, but he has an older brother who committed suicide in their sister's house, great family gift, there is no denying it! He was either autistic or bipolar).

My father could be considered more of a narcissist but with high IQ, almost a genius, but who misused his potential. Let's say he put that skill in the service of evil. Pursuit of money and wickedness in all its forms. In addition, because I reminded him of his mother, he was stricter with me. He despised her even though she was a truly wonderful woman, whom I really adored, in short, he resented her for being a bastard child, and he certainly suffered, he was born during the 2nd world war, so yeah, we can say that there were some extenuating circumstances, she thought that her husband was dead, she was alone with two children and illiterate. So, she did as she could at a time when there was neither CAF nor anything (even less support in ex-Yugoslavia), a vulnerable woman, no need to paint a picture for you, but my father with his narcissism could only see the wrong she had done him... By the way this is often how we recognize people with narcissistic disorder, I've studied this subject so much, I could talk about it for hours or more.

So, why I haven't talked about [the diagnosis] much, it's because I didn't want to feel trapped by it, I weighed up the pros and cons a lot, wondered if it would bring something positive or negative, for example at the time I passed my driving license in Arles, I was told that autistic people could only drive alone in the car but I knew that if I passed my license it was mainly to be able to take my daughter to her care, etc., I could not afford to get caught, because I am a good driver and attentive, I only take the wheel if I am sure I can drive without risk of exhaustion or crisis, I am rather master of myself, but I don't take the risk or at least, if I have no choice, I take regular breaks, like on the day I moved out of Arles.

The day before I moved out, I could not sleep because of the narcissistic owner who had rented out the ground floor of his mansion (I occupied the entire 2nd floor, he was on the 1st) but on the ground floor there were two rooms and to torture me, he rented them out to a group of young people who had parties until way too late at night and as there is police corruption here and this guy probably had friends in the Police, they did not come to see the nuisance), all night until 5am I could not sleep, I had to drive with just 2 hours of sleep since the movers came at 7am (because it was summer and it was very hot). So, being a new driver I had to pause every hour, I was very scared, but I was careful, and as soon as I felt signs of fatigue, I took breaks. So I really did not want to be hindered [by a diagnosis] and in any case my problem was not on the side of my employability since my high intellectual potential gives me rather good work and adaptation skills. It is really more on a sensory level that I am more fragile, social situations and relationships with others. But for that, there are not adjustments offered on the work place. It is more for yourself to know that you're not made for certain professions where you're too exposed or there are relationships that are too intense. So we have to choose a career that's less to do with others.

The impact of saying my diagnosis or not, I think is mainly in the difficulty of being able to be natural in my relationships with others. It's difficult to make friends, whether to tell them and when, I told my man quickly on the first day we met, because in fact, he was one of the movers in Toulouse, I had hired a small family business and one of them was him. We talked a lot while they were packing my things (I had such a hard time with my previous moves and I had a few, that I decided to take advantage for once of the moving allowance from the Council, in relation to my daughter), and he had a lot of compassion for the fact that I was alone, with my daughter, her disability is more obvious and it touched him. So he even came back to help me put up furniture that I bought from Ikea, and then he said shyly how he felt and hey, it happened spontaneously without any calculating or anything. We will have been together for 2 years next September. Everyone told us that we got together too quickly, but against all odds, despite the ups and downs, we have gotten to know each other and we love each other. It is not easy every day, because he is not savvy in couple relationship or family issues. He also has an atypical profile, maybe like ADHD. So we learn a lot from one another.

It's not easy not to talk about it, but at the same time, not talking about it allows me to avoid being stigmatized and not to 'lock' myself into a victim role in society. Because yes I am [a victim], especially when you know that I was mistreated and that nothing was done to help and protect me, my family, my parents' friends, all said that I must be a difficult child, even if it was in fact more the opposite, I was so unassuming that even the little I showed, my parents still used it against me. So, no, I do not want to tell my life to an authority, if one day I have to take the step it will be if one day my childhood trauma becomes too much to bear. But otherwise, no. For the moment, the confinement [due to the coronavirus] means that I keep my feelings mostly to myself and after that, then I want to move to the countryside, so far from the city that I don't have to force myself to be exposed to the public. And I'll be with the family that I built with my man, they know that I am autistic and they support me. I have a good relationship with my man's cousin, brother and brother's wife. They are kind. There is only one person in his family with whom I clash and that's his sister. Even his mother is adorable, but she lives in Tunisia.

**What are your thoughts about the autistic characters in TV series and movies?**
*Atypical*, I liked it a lot, *The Big Bang Theory* I like it a lot, but it's a bit cliché. *Rain Man* is endearing but still too cliché, but that said, there are some people like him.

I think a more ordinary life would have made him someone less fixed to routine and more open in his mannerisms in general. The other shows I didn't watch too much.

There is also the character of John Cage in *Ally Mc Beal*[18] who is really touching and whom I love very much, sincerely I would have liked to meet a man like him. I'm not saying mine is not good, but I mean I would have suffered less in my life if I had met someone like him earlier in my life. It's pretty good, but when you mix genres like in *Dexter*[19], a series I really love, or *Criminal Minds*[20], I find it harms autistic people to use too many clichés. But I really liked the movie *Temple Grandin*[21], I identified with her except not in the way she speaks. I

---

[18] Ally McBeal is an American legal comedy-drama television series (1997- 2002). Created by David E. Kelley, the series stars Calista Flockhart in the title role as a lawyer working in the fictional Boston law firm. The character John Cage is eccentric and seems to have some autistic traits, though it is never confirmed.

[19] Dexter is an American crime drama mystery television series (2006-2013). The series centers on Dexter Morgan (Michael C. Hall), a forensic technician, who leads a secret parallel life as a vigilante serial killer, hunting down murderers who have slipped through the cracks of the justice system.

[20] Criminal Minds is an American police procedural crime drama television series (2005-2020). It follows a group of criminal profilers who use behavioral analysis and profiling to investigate crimes and find perpetrators. One of the team Spencer Reid (Matthew Gray Gubler), is gifted and considered to have Aspergers, although this is never confirmed by the producers of the show.

[21] Temple Grandin is a 2010 American biographical drama film directed by Mick Jackson and starring Claire Danes as Temple Grandin, an autistic woman whose innovations revolutionized practices for the humane handling of livestock on cattle ranches and slaughterhouses.

don't have a speech impediment any more now. When I was little I was dysphasic[22]  and invented a language of my own.


**What would you like to say to someone wondering if they might be autistic?**

I would encourage them to read on the subject, read other people's accounts, maybe write their own account. I would help and encourage them and possibly help them consider another direction if there were signs of another type of disorder. I have already informed and helped a lot of people, I have contributed to two diagnoses.

To embark on a quest to conquer oneself fearlessly, that it is a fabulous epic journey. I have had many fruitless paths and ups and downs in the aftermath of the diagnosis, but I also had to deal with a life of mistreatment from my parents, and the rest of the family who looked away etc. So, as part of my journey I had a lot of things that came up to the surface. But it's always a great experience between yourself and yourself. Even if it does not follow an MDPH [official] recognition, I did not want it. I don't want to be obstructed and be told that I am sick. I am not. But it did allow me to stop my family saying that I was schizophrenic, paranoid, etc. Suddenly, I could prove that they really did not know anything and that they

---

[22] Dysphasia: One in a group of speech disorders in which there is impairment of the power of expression by speech, writing, or signs, or impairment of the power of comprehension of spoken or written language also known as aphasia.

should stop coming up with ill-informed diagnoses. It can make silly and mean people shut up. That, in itself, feels good.

From there, knowing you're autistic enables you to build yourself and move on, I can afford myself this luxury now, without it I could not have become myself, in fact I might have been unhappy my whole life without it.

# Michel

•

55 years old
Male
Belgian, lives in Belgium
Officially assessed at age 44

•

Hi! My name is Michel and I am autistic.

Have I always felt different? YES, definitely! Since when? Always! But beware, my position on this evidence has not always been the same. The diagnosis at 44 (just after that of my son and shortly before that of my daughter) was a pivotal moment. Before, I thought of approaching the borders of autism without being part of it. I wrote about it in a presentation text in my twenties. I was talking about "a childhood on the border of autism"! What I didn't know at the time was that I was actually on the other side of this border. And not slightly!

I realize I was different based on everything! Or almost. But that's not why I accepted it. No! It generated an internal conflict which would not be resolved until much later. With the diagnosis, in fact.

In what neuropsychologists call "executive functions", I fluctuate! It all depends on my general condition. I can go from hyper efficient to largely defective. The in-between is rather rare! An exception however: when in one of my specific fields, I generally find my bearings. When this is no longer the case, it is when dysfunction gets serious!

Sensory peculiarities? Special sensitivities? Certainly yes! My hearing is particularly receptive to details and generally sensitive to noise. I repeat: to noise. Music, even at a relatively high volume, causes me less problems due to its predictability. But mainly, some sound conditions pose a major problem to me (level, compression, distortion). The only solution then is to protect myself by running! I got an active noise canceling headset and it became an essential tool for my travels.

The other senses? Same! Smell, taste, are very sensitive as well as touch. I can easily blind recognize objects, aromas, flavors. On a visual level, anarchy in movements and certain lighting (intensity, type of lights ...) bother me. I can distinguish different shades of colors or intensities which sometimes lead to hyperstimulation.

But what literally explodes everything else is emotional sensitivity! I am much more sensitive in this regard. Most of the time, I don't express it very much because I quickly realized that it was not really socially accepted, which gave rise to situations that were difficult to manage. In addition, even if I am very receptive to emotional states in others, I am unable to use this information to regulate my behavior in society. It has however become a working tool in my teaching and coaching practice.

However, it is rather difficult for me to name and describe my emotions: they are rather states, physical sensations that I evoke then. I have not had the opportunity to associate words with my feelings which are often very different from those of others.

Generally speaking, I need precision, accuracy, truth. My tolerance is quickly dented as soon as one departs even slightly from my bearings. But it is also very dependent on my general condition. When I'm not well, I'm much more sensitive. The feeling of insecurity can become really problematic. This obviously generates a lot of misunderstanding. So, I usually have to take care of myself or find a focus that stabilizes me. A piano, an animal, a computer that need maintenance... Otherwise, it is difficult for me to stay compensated. Fortunately, over time, the bearings have become more numerous, but it still happens that I find myself in a halt and then it can become torture.

When it comes to hygiene, I'm quickly bothered by body odor, the feeling of dry mouth or clumpy teeth. I always have a toothbrush with me, because the stimulation stemming from the feeling of deposit on or between the teeth can become haunting, taking up a good part of my attentional faculties.

My hobbies? Do I really have any? Everything I touch, I do it thoroughly! It's all or nothing! Rather than leisure, I would speak of specific interests. And they can be very specific and very invasive! This allowed me to become a true specialist in a whole series of heterogeneous fields which go from linguistics to music, sound recording, arc welding, bicycle mechanics, computing... In general self-taught, with sometimes more "academic" interludes.

My "hobbies" are not hobbies. They take on a dimension that is far too important, they express an interest that is far too deep to stick to that label. No, these are real centers of interest that can be devouring. But ultimately, through each of them, isn't the passion for optimization, search for better operation, the common thread? The very thread that I have always sought for myself, in fact.

What developments have I seen? An acuity which increased with awareness, but also a greater acceptance of my particularities since the diagnosis. I stopped fighting myself, wanting to be like everyone else. It's way too exhausting! And then, was it not in my particularities that I found a way to integrate myself, to make myself useful? Oh, certainly still in a very imperfect way, but I know that there is no going back. I prefer to succeed in my life as an autist than to do everything like the others but not as well!

As per my professional path, I'm looking for it, actually! Oh, I did work. But officially (with remuneration), very little for my age. I have been a Spanish teacher, but not in my region, no, in the German-speaking Community of Belgium. For 16 years. And I don't speak German! My status was not "classic" either: derogation of title required. Yes, I did not have the officially recognized title. Skills? Apparently yes! My pupils have achieved excellent results and the Spaniards have always had a hard time believing that I was not at least of Spanish origin. But there you go, my career has never been able to formalize due to my "atypical" path. So I found myself back at my starting point. I then went back to school at 52 years old and started a specialization as a coach in school environments. I am therefore currently a "young student" looking for professional integration.

I am currently a coach in school environments following a specialization recently offered in the course. This allowed me to formalize a process that has been built continuously from the age of 12 to now. Why? It seems obvious: this is what I have always done and which allowed me to get there feeling useful and to legitimize the fact that I was born different. I do what I do as I do BECAUSE I am as I am. It remains for society to allow the "different" to act differently. Failing which, it will be futile or abusive to speak of inclusion.

**How and when did you make the connection between you and autism?**
The diagnosis itself occurred late in my life. But the intuition of difference appeared very quickly. At first, associated with the denial and difficulty of feeling other, elsewhere. I wanted to fit in, to be part of the family, the group, the society, but! It regularly stuck and I experienced harassment, mistreatment, mutual misunderstandings. In short, it was not easy. On a purely academic level, it was going pretty well. In terms of integration, it was just the opposite. At 12, the conflict crystallized: school results or integration? It

was then that I had the inspiration to start accompanying the learning difficulties of my comrades. The "cruddy nerd with glasses" then became for some people a resource person. This allowed me to acquire status, at least partially. But that was not bad for a start. For the rest, the difficulties continued. Communication remained problematic and the discrepancy manifest. It was a little later that I started music and piano. Revelation: it finally allowed me to communicate emotions, feelings. Music has become a refuge. It offered me a place as an accompanist in a choral and instrumental group. However, there too, it stuck. I was very demanding, even intransigent on the quality of the services and I did not adhere at all to the amateur and good-natured side of this first group. So I left it to join a baroque song ensemble. The reduced staff and the very "specialist" side of the approach would suit me more. However, the questions remained. It was a little later that I was going to ask myself more openly the question of difference and that I was going to mention autism for the first time. I had been asked as a sound engineer for a project to set Mallarmé's poems to music by the composer. She asked me to provide a text to explain my particular approach to sound recording. I then openly used the term "autism" in connection with this approach. It is difficult not to recognize a posteriori the association between the perception of a difference and the intuition of its origin.

**Did you seek an official assessment?**
Although the diagnosis brought me a better balance, it did not eliminate all difficulty! That would be too good.

I do not regret having gone there. Never. I even think that everyone, whatever their neurodevelopmental profile, should seriously consider this essential question: "Who am I?" » Not in a limiting, confining way, but on the contrary to better understand their difficulties, as well as discovering and expressing their potential. What weighs on me right now is not autism per se: I know it defines me, it makes me who I am, it enables what I can do so well. No, what weighs on me is the social pressure exerted on everyone to get into a sort of mold which turns out to be rather abusive for a growing number of people. Among these, a number of women who will often find it even more difficult to have their peculiarity recognized, who will be blamed for not managing to do what others do...

## Are you aut?

Well, I think if I mentioned it directly on my CV, it is because I am not hiding it! Here are the exact terms I use: "A de facto school coach since the age of 12, I have many other talents that may, at first glance, seem heterogeneous. Do not trust appearances and do ignore prejudice. I have a neurodevelopmental particularity which is also my major asset: I am autistic (Asperger), which gives me a particular outlook that I like to share with people different from me. My journey, more than training, is above all punctuated with experiences and meetings".

"Do you have to say you are autistic?" "I had to answer that question, especially during my thesis at the end of my training specialization. Here is the answer I gave: if

I do not mention it, I see in my interlocutor accumulate marks of astonishment or reactions which show me that there is in him the perception of a particularity, but the interpretation that will be made of it will almost never be that of autism. If I allow this situation to continue, my discomfort increases and when finally I have to talk about it, I am then no longer able to do it or it's very difficult. So, most of the time, I don't take long to bring up the subject, as soon as something a little too prominent appears.

### What are your thoughts about the autistic characters in TV series and movies?

There's some good, some relatively good, some not so good and some very bad! The main interest of autism in movies and series is that it's being exposed. The trouble is that it is done most often in a caricatured manner. They "have to" make autism visible by exaggerating most of the time. In addition, depending on the outputs, other mistakes are conveyed such as the confusion between autism and psychosis, for example. *Rain Man* is considered by many to be the archetype of the autistic. However, Kim Peek, who served as a model for the character played by Dustin Hoffman in the film, was not autistic, but had deficient features in the brain morphology: he lacked the corpus callosum and his cerebellum was damaged. This association between *Rain Man* and autism also contributes to perpetuating the myth of the autistic scholar - who exists but is not the norm. The revolution would be to present an autistic character played by an autistic actor. But no doubt it would be less spectacular. However they did it with Down syndrome, so it should be possible for autism ...

### What would you like to say to someone wondering if they might be autistic?

When someone evokes the hypothesis of being autistic, or just wonders about it, I always stay extremely careful. I think this is not a path to be considered lightly, because the consequences can be disruptive or even destabilizing.

In addition, being part of a multidisciplinary team that receives people asking this question or having had to ask it, I am experienced in the practice of differential diagnosis. If I can have intuitions, impressions, these need to be corroborated by more systematic investigations. The time invested in this process then leaves time to tame this reality gradually. This allows a better integration of the identity dimension linked to this eventuality. The goal is not only to answer yes or no to the question asked, but also and above all to bring the elements of well-being, better self-acceptance, and a more respectful personal development.

A conclusion to all of this? I don't think one is born different by chance. Isn't spending loads of energy to be like everyone else, but not as good, the opposite of evolution?

# Kayla

•

29 years old
She/her pronouns
American, lives in the USA
Self-assessed

•

Ever since I can remember, I knew I was different from everyone around me. When I was around eight years old, I started to believe I was an alien. It wasn't a delusion, but a response to my feelings of not fitting in or being able to understand the behavior of my friends. In my young mind, I couldn't convince myself that I wasn't profoundly different than others and that led me to question my own humanity. I was passionate about things no one seemed to understand, I had a very intricate way of playing, I was incredibly creative and developed a special interest in performing. My daily life was spent pretending to fit in with others, and always masking my personality with another.

My hobbies and special interests are almost far too many to name. I have a profound love of theater and singing that has lasted me my whole life. I have also had a large amount of crafty special interests. I used to go through phases of sculpting, painting, knitting etc., before I discovered quilling which has been my main hobby and talent for several straight years. I make paper jewelry that is actually quite beautiful and sell it when I can. I am also a major science and political nerd, watching lectures and several hours of news every day. My newest special interest is gardening and learning how to grow things I can use. Food, tea, medicine.... I love learning about plants. My special interests are my reason for living.

I am currently unemployed because my nannying job is no longer available since the Coronavirus happened. I've spent most of my working life in childcare because I seem to have a knack for understanding and nurturing kids. Thankfully I have my parent support right now. I don't know what I would do without a job if they weren't here for me.

**How and when did you make the connection between you and autism?**
I was 21 when I was first gifted a book by Temple Grandin. *"Thinking in Pictures"* was life changing for me to read. Never before had I read a book by an author who actually thinks and experiences things in the way I did. I literally believed I was the only person who thought and functioned in this way. I knew then I was autistic... I then began to read half a dozen other books by autistic authors, just to make sure, and it was mind blowing how many aspects of my life were connected to this one neurological difference. It was bittersweet because I had to wait 21 years before I finally got the tools to understand myself, but I am so glad I now have the knowledge now.

**Did you seek an official assessment?**

When my parents and I learned I was on the spectrum, it made just as much sense to them as it did me, and they were very supportive in helping me assert my self-diagnosis. About 2 years ago, my parents wanted me to see if I could get a formal assessment. My primary care doctor believed I might be on the spectrum and referred me to a psychiatrist who told us he couldn't diagnose me as an adult or didn't feel qualified. I asked for recommendations, and spent weeks calling professionals in my very small state and none of them gave me more than another referral... My family then saw a counselor who we wanted to connect us to someone who would evaluate me, but so far we have no luck. All we need is to find a single person willing to see me, but it seems impossible at this point. Many of these diagnosis capable doctors are not covered by my insurance and if we did find one I may not be able to afford it anyway.

Not being diagnosed has really messed up the first 18 years of my life... I was struggling with learning disabilities and when the school didn't test me, my mother took me for testing at a private facility. They spent 8 hours over two days only to say that I have an "unknown learning disability". I got no help, and the depressed creature I became back then is something I wouldn't wish on my worst enemy. Now that I know why I am the way I am, I can regulate myself better.

**Are you aut?**

I am extremely open about my autism. I don't want to be ashamed anymore and it helps me be more understood.

**What are your thoughts about the autistic characters in TV series and movies?**

I am sick of the stereotype of white upper-middle-class or higher-class autistic boys and men repeatedly being used in the media to portray autistics.... Most of us did not have the advantages and financial means to make ourselves into the successful or inspiring geniuses most of these characters portray. Where are the television shows about the autistic girl in middle school and has no idea why she's so different? Or just any kind of autistic female character is almost nonexistent and that's an outrage.

On the bright side, there is a female artistic character on a show called *Better Things* and I think that they are doing a really good job showing how complex and difficult being a teen girl on the spectrum is, without making her autism the focal point of the entire show. I hope shows like that get more common.

**What would you like to say to someone wondering if they might be autistic?**

I would say, first of all you are not alone. You may be feeling a lot of internalized ableism or denial, or maybe you're fully embracing the possibility that you may have been on the spectrum all along.... Whatever your current state, know that there are countless other people who have been exactly where you are. I suggest reading books by autistic authors, seek advice and input from autistic adults and make yourself at home in our community. It is better to research and seek guidance from autistics before trying to get diagnosed, because you may find out it's not worth the process.

The autistic community will embrace you if you discover you're one of us. Always.

# Lilith

•

33 years old
Gender-non-conforming female
Swiss, lives in Switzerland
Officially assessed at age 32

•

I felt different early on, the first memory I can remember was from 3 years old. There were other little girls around 3 to 5 years old playing in a neighborhood playground and they organically knew how their play worked, they passed toys as if they just knew what the other was about to do and they talked about these things that didn't make sense to me, except that I felt that I wanted to belong but when I tried to join in, everything I did seemed to be the wrong thing to do and they got cross with me.

Over time, I tried to (still at age 3!) find out what it was that made me not belong, and I even insisted on being baptized because I formed the belief that that was why I was different, after asking other kids and they just happened to have the discussion of who was baptized and their families had told them how an important thing that was and they told me that somehow that was something that was needed. Also there I noticed that the other kids definitely had other thought processes, because they did not THINK about those things like I did, they just seemed to repeat what was told at that point.

It has been the same feeling experience for me in a lot of scenarios ever since and it led to a lot of really hurtful bullying as I was not really able to discern until a later age what social cues were made and what was said in earnest and what as a tease or bad joke and what their neurotypical meaning underneath was. The only times in my life where I did feel belonging and that I was welcome as I am and that I did everything right and that I was able to pick up on how to create an energetic flow and interpersonal harmony turned out to be with people who either were diagnosed autistic already or turned out later to be autistic and a few people with ADHD.

In terms of hobbies, I didn't feel like I stood out a lot as a child but now I do seem to have interests in things that don't appeal to the majority of people together with ones that are quite common. Like, when I want to know something I REALLY want to know it into all the details and that seems to not be the case for most people.

Having to juggle university and jobs to keep myself living was the point where executive dysfunction and a difference in what is possible on a professional path for me became apparent, I just couldn't cope with the stress of it all plus the stress of all the trauma I had gone through previously in addition and burned out. I just couldn't do what other people managed and I settled for a mediocre job I didn't really like as a shop vendor, before burning out again later and applying for disability which was granted but that was before I was diagnosed autistic, it was for PTSD but now I am quite happy with the arrangement in regards to my needs as an autistic too.

Also, the sensory/sensitivity difference was quite noticeable to me too, I'd say since 12 years old. The other kids just didn't hold their ears with their hands when something was too loud, and when I came to high school that difference became more obvious to me as I could handle less and less stimulus together with the increasing stress from school and more bullying. The sensory difference has only evolved to become more stark as I grew older. Whether that's because I have trained myself to become even more sensitive to my own feelings and don't bulldoze myself anymore through discomfort, or whether it is because of some other reason I don't really know.

About special interests of mine I can say that I tend to hyper focus on something for a while until all the information that is there to be absorbed has been taken in and either there is not more available that isnt a repetition, or there is a feeling of satisfaction with the interest, and then I move to the next thing... I was like that for as long as I can remember. There were phases of interests that lasted longer or stayed, but I tend to focus on a thing and memorize what I can or participate in the activity as long as it feels good, and then try the next thing that captures my attention. And there are so many interesting things on this world, I doubt I will ever be bored...

Maybe my special interest is just understanding everything :D

My hobbies, I would say are art, as in painting and drawing myself and hiking/being in nature and doing "witchy stuff"/herbalism are those that I always loved.

I am not employed, I get disability allowance since I sought out treatment for PTSD.

## How and when did you make the connection between you and autism?

I am not quite sure how to answer that. I am not sure at this point whether my mother had gotten a diagnosis for me when I was a child and just didn't tell me, there was some discussion about sending me to a special needs class that was really confusing to me and shady at the time, when I was 8 years old. I was definitely for myself late diagnosed with 32 years of age, after I had seen a documentary about women on the spectrum and kind of connected the dots because I am/was friends with several autistic people all my teenage and adult life and I finally saw it in myself too. I mean, now it seems kind of obvious looking back, but I needed to find out slowly I guess and release the resistance to it imposed on me by negative societal judgements and ableism. I had known autism existed a long time before, and I was told also by a counsellor who helps unemployed people work out what job they might be good at it might be good for me to be assessed for autism, but at the time (I was 23 years old) it seemed like the thing that would make it impossible for me to find a job and have an independent life which I desperately wanted. When I finally had a safe life in terms of income and housing, I was finally prepared to let the awareness sink in.

I do have PTSD as a co-condition, but was misdiagnosed by someone who didn't even care to talk with me for more than 5 minutes as having borderline personality disorder, which I definitely don't have.

**Did you an official assessment?**
I did, yes.
I thought it would be a good outside confirmation, I made it mean that I was not crazy, just different :) and it definitely helps with the disability income to have it official.

In Switzerland it's not that difficult to get an assessment and the waiting time isn't that long either, I waited maybe 2 months tops after my psychotherapist referred me, and the cost is covered by health insurance. The assessment itself was not that difficult either, but I was under a lot of stress from having my whole self-image and sense of self shaken up, and going places with trains - which I had to do for it - is a challenge for me too sensory wise. I found the part where you have to look at pictures of pairs of eyes and determine what expression they convey probably the most challenging part of the whole testing, but this is supposed to be difficult if you are autistic.

**What are the consequences on your health/balance of having an official assessment?**
Mostly, peace of mind and self-acceptance have had a huge beneficial impact on my health. Of course the

integration phase was long, a lot to process and I did a lot of retrospective puzzle-piecing-together, but that is a normal part of becoming aware of your identity... I would say now a year later I have integrated this part of myself quite well and have now a lot better understanding of what is good for me and what isn't and can structure my life better with that in mind, and I have gained so much more compassion for myself (internally). It is ultimately a great relief.

**Are you aut?**
Yes.
I don't see why I should hide who I am, I did that for too long and it didn't do me that much good. Although, I don't go out and just shout it around, but if it comes up in conversation with people I feel ok to tell, I will say it.
It goes beyond just telling close friends. I do have the privilege to not have to go to work, I don't know if I'd be comfortable sharing it in a work environment depending on where and in what position though. But in my private life, I share it quite liberally.

Some people understand me better for telling it, and some understand themselves better for it.

**What are your thoughts about the autistic characters in TV series and movies ?**
I haven't watched all of them. I like the series Atypical, Sam is an interesting individual but in no way representing of all autistics, it is a nice story though

portraying his and his family's navigation through social life challenges, although it bothered me so much that his best friend was such a sexist influence on him. The Big Bang Theory was funny to begin with, but got annoying quite quickly and it really made me angry how Sheldon is treated sometimes and how his behaving in an "autistic way" is made to be the point of jokes. And to see all the dysfunctions from all the characters actually.

Rain Man is kind of a trigger subject for me, my mother loved that movie and found it so genius (I have shut her out of my life because being in contact with her is not healthy for me), I tried to re-watch it last year because it is after all about an autistic, but I couldn't, because of all the insensitivity portrayed and how no one is able to or willing to attune to/ have empathy with the autistic character (or also, with other NT's...). Like, don't people see how much pain they are causing him? Yeah I couldn't watch the whole movie.

**What would you like to say to someone wondering if they might be autistic?**

Women on the spectrum mostly defy all stereotypes that are repeated in broad society about autism, which are mostly based on how boys present. And being autistic is not that horrible tragedy, it's just a way a person with a brain can be, it's just one of a vast variety of different neurological setups, and knowing your setup can bring so much self-understanding and self-acceptance and opens the doors to finding places and people who really resonate and meeting your needs better.

If you already wonder whether you might be autistic, you probably did have challenges in your (especially social) life that made you question yourself, be brave to see yourself and find out who you are, with all the ways that feel right to you.

And dare look beyond concepts society has told you about autism. You might just find the people you belong with.

# Emily

•

20 years old
Female
British, lives in England
Officially diagnosed at age 13

•

I was never a stereotypical child. In many ways I think I have always been "different", but it was late primary school and the start of high school where I really noticed it. One thing that I have always done is collect things. When I was young and one of the first signs to my mum was, I was collecting frube[23] yogurt packets. I have had so many collections in the past including: train tickets, rubbers, notebooks, pens and pencils, cards and many other things. I know that to some people this may seem like a normal, typical behavior but where most people might collect small amounts mine is very "obsessive almost".

Another thing is that I now know is different is how immensely sensitive I really am. One thing for me is the feel of certain textures such as velvet or sponge, when I feel or have had to feel them it's  this emotion of sharpness down me and my ears feel like they are in so much pain, it to me feels like physical hurt.

---

[23] a squeezable yogurt brand in the UK, which packaging has different faces on.

Temperature is another sensory issue I struggle a lot with. When I was younger I didn't feel temperature very well at all and my mum would have to check the bath as even though it had no cold in I couldn't feel the heat. I am now getting better with trying to regulate heat but it is still a work in progress.

I am very much a creature of habit and I am very routine bound; without routine I find it very hard to cope. I like to wear a lot of the same kinds of clothes mainly leggings and a long t shirt I can't stand to feel claustrophobic in clothes, so I like to stick with what I know I feel comfortable in.

I am a highly creative person and love art. I draw almost daily and draw in a lot of details. I do feel my autism has a big part to play in my art and how I see things. I'm able to notice patterns and detail where others may not.

I also love poetry to express my inner emotions and feelings.

I'm a big Disney fan and collector. I'm especially obsessed with Alice in wonderland, I really relate to the story and characters.

I also love helping people. Especially people who maybe struggle with communicating or just need a friend. I feel autism helps me understand people and resonate with people who have a hidden disability like me. Sometimes people just need a little patience and understanding which I really try do for people.

I currently attend a specialist college for people with disabilities which I love! And I am working with them to make my own art business. I also sell my artwork through their shop.

## How and when did you make the connection between you and autism?

Throughout school I always struggled academically and socially, I was always bottom of the class. I was tested many times for dyslexia, but it never came back that I had it. I was known to CAMHS since being 8 but they never did anything really. I was a very anxious child in school and used to always rip my hair out (which I now know can be an autism trait). Hence why I went to see CAMHS.

But it was my mum at the time who was online and saw an article about Asperger's syndrome (my official diagnosis). Asperger's wasn't as known back then and my mum said when she read it, it just summed me up. I was going through assessment for a long time which Is the case for most young people in the UK. Before being diagnosed I started suffering badly with mental health and only then was I diagnosed when it got to a point a professional had to step in and I was diagnosed. I remember the day because I was ill for that appointment so my mum went on her own (I did not know this would be the day I would find out). My mum came home, and I was laid on her bed feeling unwell and she said you have Asperger's it's official or something along them lines. It was a weird feeling and I had not really read much at all about it.

Now at 20, I have learnt so much about myself and others on the spectrum. And looking back on my younger self I can really identify aspects of my life that at that time I did not understand.

Masking is also such a big part to play in my late diagnosis and the person I am. Although I still do mask I do without knowing a lot I think just being aware is helpful.

**Did you seek an official assessment?**

I have an official diagnosis from CAMHS of Asperger's Syndrome.

It was an exceptionally long and difficult process. For 13 years I had learnt the art of masking and so getting a diagnosis was incredibly difficult because I was almost playing the role of a stereotypical teenager to try fit in.

I personally am glad I have an official diagnosis, but I do feel if I had had it before high school, I may have had a lot less issues than I did and still have now. The thing for me is it helps me understand and when people say "you aren't autistic" or " you don't look autistic", I know that it is a professionals word which helps me feel more at peace. I think it answered a lot of questions for me and helped me understand why I am a little different and why I may experience different things in different ways. In some way it gave me a peace of mind almost a feeling that it's not all just in my head and that it is a real thing and there are other people who are like me.

**Are you aut?**

I would say yes I am openly autistic with people if I feel it's in a suitable situation and setting. I do not feel the need to hide my autism and often share things on social media to help educate people. I've also done a lot of campaigning to help people with disabilities in the education system and have a Facebook page dedicated to helping spread positivity about autism.

I think with everything there sometimes may be small negatives but for me being open about being autistic has helped me so much. I'm able to help other people like me and show people that autism shouldn't be stereotyped. I always welcome people to ask me questions as I'm a person first and foremost and autism is just a part of me, but it isn't me. I feel awareness and education is the key to a more accepting world. I would rather someone ask me about it rather than ignore me or judge me for it.


**What are your thoughts about the autistic characters in TV series and movies?**
I have watched all of Atypical and I did enjoy it. Autism is a spectrum and I do feel any show or film will have people saying that is not autism but as we know autism is a spectrum and can be presented in many ways. As with any how it is going to have an element of drama to get people watching it but I enjoyed it a lot. I liked that it did not just show the main autistic characters struggles but also how the parents feel about it all and his sister. The other thing about the show is it has got people talking about autism who maybe hadn't even known about it etc so I think that in itself is amazing. Sure, it's not 100% but as far as the show goes I enjoy it and think it had been done and portrayed well.

I haven't watched any other programs really with autism characters apart from a show in the UK called the A word which is about a young boy with autism.

**What would you like to say to someone wondering if they might be autistic?**

If you do feel you might be autistic my opinion would be to do some research and maybe see if you feel you resonate with the text a bit. But I would also advise that not every information on the internet on autism is factual and truthful so try stick to proper informational guides. If you're looking for a proper diagnosis, going to a doctor is your best bet and telling them etc and they will point you in the right direction.

I think it's so important that people remember autism does not define you or who you are. It is merely a part of you. If being self-diagnosed gives you relief and comfort, then I feel that is valued just as much as an official diagnosis to you.

Most of all just be you.

# Kelebek

•

29 years old
Female
Turkish, lives in Turkey
Self-assessed

•

I started to feel different when I began primary school. I couldn't understand how quickly other children made friends and formed groups. But it was mostly okay, because I had cousins and a sister, so I wasn't completely lonely.

Although I remember one specific memory very clearly. I was 8 and was going to a place after school, something like a kindergarten but for older children. There were a bunch of kids my age and we used to stay there until our parents come from work and pick us up. The feeling of being different started to bother me because I couldn't make any friends there, also bullying started and it was unbearable. I remember the day where I looked out from the window and wanted to die, because I was clearly unwanted and unlovable. I was thinking I deserve that, because that was the age when white lies begin for typical children, and it was actually normal, so I also did that. But it felt horrible because of my devotion to the truth. So, I kinda thought that I'm a liar and God saw that, and he punished me by making me different (I was religious back then).

103

My sensory sensitivities were always there, but never caused any serious problems because I didn't use to explode like boys. I used to cry and grownups used to act like I'm just a picky eater or a spoiled child. So I learnt to suppress my discomforts. Because "I should do so".

Like I said, it wasn't a big problem until the bullying, because I didn't have any desire to make more friends. I had my cousins and my sisters and that was enough. I just wanted them to leave me alone. When bullying started, I started to question "Why me?" and that's when I realized because I was simply different. I translated it as "wrong", I was "wrong" somehow, but couldn't identify how and why. When bullying started to get serious, I started to be unwilling to go to school in the mornings. My parents intervened by talking to those children, cliché conversations like "It's wrong to be mean to your friend, you shouldn't do that." Mostly it didn't work, sometimes it worked and they stopped, but never accepted me as a "friend".

When this didn't work, my parents changed their mind and they started to say maybe MY behavior is wrong, sometimes I'm rude. I never understood why I was rude, because never intended to be. Now I assume it was because I didn't always say the most appropriate things.
They said I wasn't very friendly and if I want my peers to like me, then I should be nicer and smile more. They encouraged me to buy presents to them, or making favors to them, even that they never reciprocate.

As an adult now, I think it's dangerously harmful when raising a child, because this made me a person who's easy to take advantage of, with poor personal boundaries. Also, when even your own family thinks you're wrong or broken, it's hard to believe you're a good person who deserves to be loved. Sometimes I thought it wasn't fair to me, but usually I believed that I deserve what I get. It was the same with romantic partners. I believed I deserve to be treated that way, I just wanted to know "why".

There was one specific abuser, (her parents were best friends with mine, also neighbors), she was the main reason for my childhood hell. She was my first friend in life then became my secret nemesis. She was a master manipulator even at the age of 6, and psychologically tortured me for years. Sometimes used other children to abuse me. And we were always together, at school, afterschool, weekends, holidays, then college. Each time when she played "nice" in front of our parents, I believed in her, like 50+ times. Then when we were alone, the same abuse, exclusion, over and over again. Nobody would believe me, and I thought that she's the person who knows me the best because of our history together.

As a result to all of those above, I was in a denial mode for years, I always thought "I have some parts of me that I need to change, and everything will be better if I just try a little more."
I never thought I have a mental illness or neurological difference until age 23. I believed that "I wasn't trying enough."

Nothing got better in high school, nor in college, only got worse. Because social rules got more complex as years goes by, and I just couldn't adapt. Couldn't even understand no matter how hard I tried. Being a teenager, then an adult (at least biologically), only worsened things, because then I also had to deal with romantic feelings, emotions. There were more serious betrayals than "hiding someone's book" and I didn't understand nor process any of them. Why someone behaves this way etc...

As I grew older, my cousins and my sister (my little social circle) started to become distant to me, they had new friends, new interests. As an adult who now knows that they're neurotypical, I know it's a completely normal period of change and doesn't mean they don't love me anymore, but as a child, I felt intensely lonely and abandoned. After that episode, I worked hard to make new friends, usually it resulted with rejection, betrayal and trauma. I kept forcing myself only to collect more traumas.

I always had executive functioning issues, I was late to school bus every single morning. I used to lose my belongings almost every day. I was blamed of being "lazy, irresponsible, selfish, inattentive" and hated myself for that every single time. Literally hated.

Executive functioning hit the bottom after middle school. Because I started to spend so much time and energy to figure out how to make friends, how to keep friends, how to have a boyfriend or should I have that at all, because everybody seems to have one, maybe I should have one to be normal... It took all my capacity.

I only had some "good" episodes, my usual functioning became a mess. This also caused me to lose my success on other areas, and led to serious depression, very low self-esteem and self-harming. Because nothing good left on me and I was full of self-hatred. I was a smart, bright and creative kid, with straight A's at every subject, I became a terrible adult student who fails at everything and just hopes not to repeat the class.

There was the feeling (it's still here sometimes) that I had this huge potential and I just wasted it. I was sick of being myself. I used to get so angry at myself, and desperately wish to be anyone but myself but couldn't. I remember I just wanted to get out of my skin, I felt like trapped in my own body. Because how someone can be so uncomfortable with who they are, create a mess without even noticing it, and still cannot change any of it?

## How and when did you make the connection between you and autism?

Before my own autism experience, I always thought of autism as an intellectual disability. Because the examples that I see were always children with severe intellectual disability. I didn't even hear something called "Asperger's Syndrome" until the age 22.

I was having depressive episodes during my relationship at that time. Everything that is so easy for other people seemed too much for me. Even being at school in time. I also struggled a lot with my relationship because I was "childish, irresponsible and not wife-material". So I was searching for some answers online, reading tons of articles. Then I saw something about "Asperger's Syndrome". Many traits were similar to mine, but there were also big differences. Like not liking hugs or touch, not making eye contact... Now I know that:

1) The checklist is mainly based on male autistic traits
2) It is a spectrum and traits vary for each autistic individual.

At that time, at age 22, I shared this only with my ex-boyfriend and he strongly disagreed. He said I just have some self-esteem issues but it will change as I grow old. Therefore I let it go. I completely forgot about it until the end of my relationship with him and a major depressive episode started.

Then I started to look for answers again, because therapy wasn't working, medication wasn't working, nothing was helping. I told it to my family, my parents denied it strongly, my sister (who was studying psychology) was hesitant about it. At that time, one of her professors recommended a movie, Temple Grandin. She said the movie is very realistic about how a person with Asperger's Syndrome would look, behave and live. So we watched it. After seeing that movie, I was convinced that I was definitely not autistic, because I was nothing like her. My speech is almost perfect and my body language is odd sometimes (like the times when I laugh to a distressing event) but most people would say I look normal, I don't "look autistic". I seek friendships and romantic relationships. Hence she was quite different than me.

Finally, at the age of 27, one night I was suicidal. I had some conflict with my cousins that day, then I came back home and argued with my parents too. And my relationship with my sister hadn't been good for years. Those were the people that I was counting on. Whenever I felt lonely, I reminded myself that I have them. That day I felt that I was not able to understand anyone in my life, not even family members that I'd known for 20+ years. And I was always misunderstood by them, even they couldn't understand me. I felt so desperate and helpless. Like I was the only one like that on Earth. I lost all the hope. I simply didn't want to live like that for more years. I felt trapped. I decided to end my life and looking for the best way to do that.

Suddenly I remembered the "autism thing". I don't know why, but it came to my mind. I decided to search for "female autism" this time, and I found many articles. And I felt like they were written my life, my experiences, my personality. It was almost the same. Then I found a Facebook group, female members only, and I joined in. The first time I read their posts, I felt like home. First time in my life I felt belonging. The more I communicate with them, the more I was sure that I am autistic.

**Did you seek an official assessment?**
I did seek and am still seeking an official dx. I had some bad experiences about it, mostly because professionals still evaluate based on male autism phenotype. And in my country the situation is worse, even the awareness almost doesn't exist. Most people don't even know what autism is.

I want an official dx because besides my family, no one believes that I'm autistic. Also, I need therapy for an autistic person. I'm still struggling about being independent, I still live with my family, unemployed and single. I need the proper support and help to thrive.

I don't even know what my rights are if I get an official dx or how it will affect my health. Because I couldn't get any information even on this subject. The main problem in my country is, you can't find an adult autism therapist. 99% of the professionals are specialized on children. I'm still searching.

**Are you aut?**
I am aut to close friends, family, and the people that I met since I know I am autistic. I'm still not aut to acquaintances. I'm planning to be completely aut if I have an official dx. The main reason for that is most people don't believe it unless it is officially diagnosed and I don't want to be seen as attention seeking.

Still, it has a huge impact on my life that I cannot describe it with words. I feel like there was a huge baggage on my shoulders my whole life and now it's gone. I know who I am and why I am the way I am. I know I'm not a broken neurotypical.
I had this intense, almost solid feeling of loneliness. Not the level of "I don't have any friends.", it was the level of "There is no one like me on Earth".
I used to listen/ read people's stories and experiences, when they said "People do X because they feel Y" or "We

all do X sometimes because it's a part of being human."
etc... I used to feel that I don't relate at all. I used to
think "Am I not human because I don't feel/think like
this at all?" Now those feelings are completely gone.
Because I know there are people, many people that I
relate to. I belong with them. I am connected to them.


## What would you like to say to someone wondering if they might be autistic?

I know it is incredibly hard not to feel broken, damaged,
excluded in a world who treats you as a failure every
day. But the truth is we just don't live in a world that's
designed for people like us. In this world we need
accommodations, patience and tolerance, more than
neurotypicals. It would be exactly the opposite if they
were the minority, don't forget that. And people who're
willing to give these to you, will already do it no matter
they know you're autistic or not.

Keep learning about autism and try to find new ways
that works for you to have a better life. Reach out to
fellow autistics. Most of my life I felt that I'm not living,
I'm just surviving. Now I see it doesn't have to be this
way and we autistics deserve a good life too. Just
surviving is not enough.

# Lucinda

•

27 years old
Female/Woman
British, lives in United Kingdom
Officially assessed

•

I always felt a little "different". I struggled to fit in from a young age, and was always the weird kid. I never really understood how I was "different", I just understood from other people that I was.
It's hard to explain how it feels.

Socially: I love having friends. As I get older, I really value quality friendships, and I'm lucky to have many friends. I love going out, and go to festivals, pubs, bars, stay in hostels, I adore meeting new people. Despite that, I struggle to know how to interact with people, which I guess is a knock-on effect from being bullied as a kid. I hate saying and doing the wrong thing, so I often second guess myself before speaking.
I definitely get on better in 1-1 situations, and groups are more challenging, which has been an ongoing struggle throughout my life. I initially put this down to social anxiety, but CBT and other methods didn't help.

Executive dysfunction: I've always struggled to get things done, even though I consider myself to be a very organised person. For example, right now I know that I need to pack my clothes away after returning from a trip. It's been 3 days, and I probably won't get around to doing it until I run out of clean clothes. Sometimes I'll be thinking "I should do this thing right now" and still not do it. For example, I'll walk past a glass and think to myself "I should put this in the dishwasher" - and whilst I'm looking at it, and thinking this, I'll still walk right past it. And I'll even be thinking to myself, "why am I not picking it up?"

But then, when I really want something, I'll find a way to get it done. I completed my undergraduate degree whilst working full time, and somehow managed to only have one late assignment in 5 years of studying. At work, I find it easy to complete all my tasks, but when it comes to some annoying admin work like appraisal forms, I struggle to force myself to do it.

Thought process: This is probably one of the biggest "differences" I see in myself and other autistic people vs neurotypicals. I always thought I was just a little bit eccentric (which I supposed is just a diplomatic word for "harmlessly weird") or missing something very obvious. For example, I don't understand why people are so obsessed with getting into work at 9am on the dot. I know being late is annoying and rude if you're meeting someone or have an appointment, or if customers or colleagues rely on you. But if I'm going to work, where I don't have to meet with or even talk to anyone until 11am, why does it matter if I get in at 9:10am? As long as I'm doing all my work and dedicating the required hours to it, it doesn't make any difference. I've asked some of my bosses and they can't answer it, just mumble something about it being the principal of it. I ask them which employee they think is happier – the one who gets reprimanded for being 5 minutes late, or the one who has flexibility and independence. I ask how they think this impacts productivity. I then ask them if there's a problem with the quality or timing of my work. They don't like those questions, but can't explain why and it definitely impacts my career.

On the plus side, I often reach logical conclusions much faster than other people. But they also don't like that, and my ideas in meetings are often met with "well it's not that simple". When I ask why, they can't answer. Eventually, it gets debated and we end up implementing that idea, after wasting a lot of time. And I rarely get credited for the solution, instead the people involved seem annoyed at me, even though I've been very professional in my suggestion (e.g "Can you think of any reason we can't implement xyz instead?"). People in general waste a lot of time drawing up obvious solutions, and I've never been able to figure out why this is.

Other people's perceptions of me is probably one of the key points too. I've always been told that I'm quiet, aloof, an ice queen, intimidating. This is ridiculous to me, as I'd say that I'm one of the most hyper-empathetic, sensitive and caring people I know. I genuinely feel pain if one of my friends is having problems, I just express it in different ways. For example, I'll obsessively Google around for solutions rather than give them a hug and say useless things like

"Oh no that sucks!". I've had to learn to say the useless things too, but it's exhausting because I run out of things to say. This isn't to say that I just bombard them with practical solutions - all my friends still come to me for advice or if they feel upset, because they say that I genuinely help, and I'm a good listener.
But I have resting bitch face, so I still get called an ice queen.

My special interests change quite often.
For a while I was obsessed with keeping hamsters and rats, and creating their environments. I'd talk about them quite a lot, and after overhearing some colleagues mocking me I joined online forums so I could have a space to discuss it with other fanatics. I learned that not everyone enjoys hearing others talk about their passions. I stopped talking in work a lot after a few incidents like that, and this is something I'm actively working on.

A shorter-lived special interest was junior doctors – I must have read so many books by doctors! I have no idea why. That lasted a couple of months.

Travel is probably my primary hobby – I love exploring new cultures and learning about the history of different countries, and seeing how this impacts their culture today. I went backpacking for 15 months and it was an absolutely incredible experience.

Since I was 9 I've been quite into coding and IT development. It started because I was obsessed with an old virtual pet website, Neopets. I wasn't very good at making popular guilds, or getting points in the games, so I figured I could just learn to make my own. That escalated, and I've continued my passion for this subject.

I'm a Data Architect/Business Intelligence Developer. I love problem solving, and it fits in quite well with my passion for coding. I'm very ambitious and adore having a career that I can consistently build on, and have been doing since I was 18. Every project is different, so I can avoid feeling like I'm in a Groundhog Day remake, and keep learning more and more. I also like that I can be part of a team, but I can also get away with not talking to anyone if I'm having an off day.

I'm planning on starting my MBA in the next couple of years, so I can aim towards a CTO position or starting my own business. Before I do that I need to improve my ability and confidence with talking to groups.

## How and when did you make the connection between you and autism?

I'm not sure. Some of my friends sometimes joked about it. One day I was struggling with relationship issues, and started googling to see if I could find someone with the same issues. I was ecstatic when I found someone who had identical problems! It was like reading my own diary. I read some more of her blog posts, and then realized that she was autistic. That surprised me, and I started researching autism. Once I educated myself, I requested a referral for an assessment. Turns out my friends weren't joking.

**Did you seek an official assessment?**
I wanted to know more. I wasn't 100% sure that I was autistic, especially as I still had the idea in my head that autistic = antisocial introvert. I also didn't want to self-diagnose myself in case I got it wrong, as I know many autistic women were initially incorrectly diagnosed with conditions like borderline personality disorder, and struggled to develop the right coping mechanisms for themselves. I didn't want to do the reverse, and miss out on finding the right answers.

For me, it was worth it. I've never been happier, and I've started to gain confidence. I know my limits, I know how to listen to my body and my mind, and I can grow into the person I should have been. I've stopped people-pleasing so much, and stopped dwelling on the awkward or inappropriate things I've said. I've also learned how to deal with social situations where I've said/done the wrong thing.

**Are you aut?**
Yes and no. If it's relevant I'll share it, for example when a colleague mentioned that their kid is having an assessment I offered some support. But much like anything, it doesn't always come up in conversation. I guess it's the same as how my natural hair colour doesn't often come up in conversation. It's just another part of being me.

I can't say that it's had much negative impact on my life. During my last project, I was struggling with lighting and noise in one specific office, and I was able to ask for reasonable accommodations so I could complete my work to a higher standard. I found that very helpful.

## What are your thoughts about the autistic characters in TV series and movies?
The only 2 I've seen are:

*Rain Man* – I haven't watched this in a long time, but I think I enjoyed the movie. This plays up to an awful lot of stereotypes, but it's an old movie so that's to be expected. Unfortunately this seems to be most people's idea of autism, and is often used as an insult.

*Atypical* – I really enjoy this series. This still plays up to a lot of stereotypes, but it's a step in the right direction and moves away from dehumanising autistic people. Sam has a friend, a loving sister, a job and a girlfriend. The Mother gets on my nerves though, she seems to base her entire identity on her sons neurotype and she's extremely self-centric.

I'd love to see a TV show portray a less stereotypical autistic person. Someone average, who has an active social life, a few hobbies, a career without being a "genius" or particularly unique, who just so happens to be autistic with a few difficulties. In essence, a show about a person who happens to be autistic, rather than a show about autism. It'd also be good to portray events from the autistic perspective – highlighting why random social rules seem so stupid, why some of us struggle with illogical thinking etc. I've fantasised about writing such a show myself, but unfortunately that's really not my forte!

**What would you like to say to someone wondering if they might be autistic?**
I'd urge them to seek an assessment, knowing has really changed my life. It can give you the answers you need to really become yourself again, and improve your quality of life.

I'd also tell them that it might seem scary and strange, but they will adjust to the idea quite quickly. Autism isn't a scary thing, awareness for it is just low. And I bet we all know a lot more autistic people than we realise (I'm pretty sure my old CEO was).

# Hanna

•

22 years old
Female
Brazilian, lives in Brazil
Officially assessed at age 22

•

I've always felt different, as long as I can remember (about 4 y.o.). I did not like to see new people, I did not find interesting to play with imaginative scenarios unless I used my "imaginary friends"- that were actually kind of characters that already existed in movies or cartoons – so I could not interact with real people. I used to have a pretty long and curly hair that would create huge knots due to my lack of understanding that I had to take care of them and combing it would cause a huge headache but I preferred doing that than having to meet people that were on my grampa's house, where I lived at 8yo. People would always tell my parents they were very lucky cause I didn't like to play outside and was very quiet, I preferred to read about space, trying to be faster in my math assignments and so on... I learned to read at 4, at home. I had a big interest in things being accurate scientifically and people would call me crazy because I would know things that were a little "too smart" for my age.

I was VERY rational and sincere, didn't really understood emotions and when I expressed them, they weren't very welcomed by my parents so I had a hard time masking until I got to my teens. Even now I'm very rational but also very in touch with my emotions and intuition. I care A LOT about details and I date a very talkative girl with not such great of a memory – mine was great, I know hundreds of songs by heart, would always help my parents to find some place they were looking for on the street because I could remember the number of the house/store/etc correctly, knew all my friend phone numbers, and so on - she always tells a story to our friends and I proceed to "correct" her with things that I know don't actually matter to the story but bother me a lot, is like: "we were eating lunch on our living room and then ..... (something a NT would find impressive)" and I go "it was brunch in our kitchen."

As far as sensitivity goes, sometimes I can barely function because everything – everything! sound, touch, smell, light... - is too much. Another days I can barely perceive stuff. Processing audio and visuals at the same time is barely impossible. I guess is the thing that nowadays sets me apart from neurotypical people the most, because is the most debilitating – along side with executive dysfunction. Hygiene it's very hard, the baseline of what is acceptable is not very clear to me, especially because I live in Brazil and people are absolutely obsessed with cleaning (not saying it lightly, it's the country with the major number of anxiety diagnosis worldwide, including but not limited to OCD); most hygiene activities take a lot of energy for me but they don't feel bad at least. And don't even get me started on executive dysfunction hahaha my brain has some self-made rules such as "if the floor is dirty it MUST be cleaned, now!" it doesn't matter if I'll burn my food, if I'll fail tests, I can't properly control it...

I still don't understand much about special interests. I obsess with many things and I don't know if they meet the criteria or not, as they appear in waves that go on and off. Nonetheless, one thing that I'm always interested is in people's height, especially famous people.

I honestly don't count it as a job but I'm a part time oraculist (reading tarot and other types of cards) and I manage part of my father's restaurant social media. It takes so little time of my life that I can't consider it a job on my opinion. I work as a volunteer intern in a company part time, but it did not end well for me, so I didn't seek for another formal job ever since.

Talking with my girlfriend the other day she said it makes so much sense that I'm autistic because there is not a single person that knows me would not say that I'm different. Just as broad as that, but also very precise hahaha, the way I speak, the way I move, the way I like stuff, everything is not typical. I could go on and on about it but is also hard to pinpoint stuff because it seems to (and it does, I guess) permeate my whole life.

## How and when did you make the connection between you and autism?

I have depression, anxiety and PTSD. Took me a long time to have a complete diagnosis but I understood that "something was off" at a very young age and had a very hard time expressing it. I started to suspect about autism when someone I've met online has just being diagnosed, I was about 12 by the time. I resonated a lot with the things they described but just ignored it because depression was my main concern at the time. It wasn't until I saw some tiktoks while quarantined with a girl who spreads information about autism in females that I started to think about it again. I ignored it once more because I worry a lot about knowing everything about me, specially mentally, and I end up identifying with many things that do not apply to me correctly. But then my girlfriend saw those tiktok and said "I think you should see them, you might identify with it". After that I spent a reasonable amount of time researching about autism in females and REALLY identified with it. I could not ignore it anymore, so I spoke about my therapist about it. At first she reacted as I expected, saying she never imagined it, that I was just very introverted (which is also true) but still accepted to read more about it and try to understand it better. The next week she said she understood, that she saw me a lot on what she read. I felt really validated and good about myself, because even knowing about my previous conditions there where many things that remained unexplained by them, and with autism I could understand and accept myself much better.

**Did you seek an official assessment?**

At first, I wanted to, but after I spoke to my psychiatrist I was very discouraged. Unfortunately, there is so much stigma around autism in Brazil and so little understanding that I just thought about how expensive and possibly frustrating it would be. I guess the main consequence is feeling like an impostor, even if it makes perfect sense for me to be that way. One thing that I struggled with was thinking about my debilities and wondering if it meant I am disable. I came to the conclusions I possibly am, as I also have PTSD, which is considered a disability in some places. That had a weight, but I am now being able to deal with in a healthy way.

**Are you aut?**

To some friends and my girlfriend. I see the biggest impact on my educations, I don't feel comfortable in coming out to my teachers, but I think my life would be easier if they understood this part of me. Another thing is the amount of help I need, that is minimal compared to others in the community but still way bigger than a NT would need; I believe it will be hard to me to ever work in a full time job because I know I will eventually meltdown and need a lot of rest that "normal" jobs don't allow and that probably means I'll be financially dependent on my father for a long time; that makes me uncomfortable. There are positive impacts as being aut to some of my friends and my gf as they know me better and understand my behaviors better, they also support me a lot.

**What are your thoughts about the autistic characters in TV series and movies?**
I don't have an opinion as I did not watch most of them.


**What would you like to say to someone wondering if they might be autistic?**
I read that neurotypical people don't wonder about it. I mostly find it to be true. So, even if it ends up not being the case of you personally being autistic, you will still know more about people that are and might learn about better ways to cope in your general life. If it happens to be the case and you are autistic, you now have much more knowledge about yourself and will probably live a better life.

# Tammy

•

32 years old
Female
British, lives in the UK
Officially assessed at age 25

•

I was different ever since I was a toddler, my mum was a nursery nurse and saw the signs of me being different then, I had a great interest with animals and dinosaurs, preferred to play on my own and I would be sensitive to sounds and other sensory inputs, especially food. When I became aware was late primary school, before we moved to secondary school, people would stop playing imaginative games with me and I was told I had an over active imagination, that's when things started to get rough for me, I was severely bullied in high school and was told by the teachers I was stupid and didn't try hard enough.

I have several hobbies and special interests, my main ones being theme and amusement parks and building costumes. I also draw, play videogames and write, most of my drawings are digital, cause I found it very relaxing to mix the colours into interesting patterns. A lot of people assume that autistic people aren't creative because we are very logical thinkers, but I don't think that's true, I've met a lot of creative people who are autistic because we think outside the box, which means we can think of stuff people might not have thought of before.

I am a safety engineer, looking at risk management and things like that in military aircraft, it's a cool job to do, not much else I can say really cause of the nature of the work I do.

## How and when did you make the connection between you and autism?
Through one of my sisters friends who has two boys on the spectrum, they noticed that I showed similar traits to them in certain circumstances, I had also been diagnosed with dyslexia and dyscalculia in college, where it was suggested that I could be on the spectrum as well, but they weren't qualified to be able to diagnose me. My mum had been fighting with the doctors for years for a diagnosis but she never really told me what it was until it was pointed out to me in college.

## Did you seek an official assessment?
I was recommended for an official diagnosis through work, my doctor at the time was trying to get me treated for social anxiety, which was part of it not the whole, so we changed doctor and my occupational health nurse pushed with a recommendation letter. The new doctor recommended it was something that we would need to look into so put me on the waiting list.

I would say it would have been difficult on my own to be able to get the diagnosis, because of the push back from my previous doctors, but after that it was fairly straightforward, and I was further diagnosed with other things too, including things linked to mobility issues I had been having previously, which was a massive relief. It was stressful for me before having an official diagnosis though, I love going to theme parks but had to arrange to take days off work because I couldn't queue at busy times, the amount of people sent me into panic attacks and that would have been the end of the day. I also had to deal with my doctors who were trying to push anything else but autism on me, and as I previously said, high school was an absolute nightmare because "I wasn't living up to my potential" as one of the teachers told my mum.

**Are you aut?**

Yep, I am openly autistic to anyone who will listen, I have started my own vlog, although there's not much to put on it right now because of the current situation, and I have a blog to, which is a bit intermittent at the moment. It has had a massive impact on my life, because I was diagnosed with other conditions such as dyspraxia, hypermobility, traits of ADHD, Sensory Processing Disorder among other things, so I could get help with everything I needed to, allowing me to continue with my hobbies and working.

**What are your thoughts about the autistic characters in TV series and movies?**

I think it depends entirely on the context and scope of the characters and the shows that they are in, some places show a very narrow view of people on the autistic spectrum, the weird, socially awkward genius being the main one. This does help point people in the right direction at times though for getting advice and information on autistic people and, if done in the right way, can benefit those on the spectrum in the long run, however some shows need to be made away that this is what autism is, a spectrum and people can be vastly different from one person to the next.

**What would you like to say to someone wondering if they might be autistic?**
To firstly work out if a diagnosis would benefit you in the long run, they take a lot to do and people do treat you differently when you are diagnosed as autistic, good and bad, I've had a few issues at work that have caused me problems, but for the most part my work have been very supportive about the whole thing.

There are places that can support you if you are undiagnosed, but if you can't get a letter from the doctor you can't get like careers pass and other things that you can be entitled to with a diagnosis.

# Dominique

•

40 years old
Female
British, lives in the UK
Self-assessed at age 36

•

When I was young I didn't know I was different, I remember being told I was weird by other children at primary school and then later at secondary school. But I didn't have a frame of reference to be able to pinpoint what that actually meant. Weird was bad, but how to be 'not weird' eluded me. I did have a few friends at primary school but I was also heavily bullied. I didn't understand the games they played and when I did join in, I seemed to take it too far. For example 'kiss chase' where the boys chased the girls to kiss them (this is not an allowable game now!) but I was genuinely scared for the girls and kept trying to 'save them' I didn't understand that they didn't want to be saved, they wanted to be caught. I'm gay now, so maybe that's why I didn't understand that. Whatever the games were, I always felt like a foreigner who didn't quite understand. The other children realised quickly that I was sometimes strange and also very gullible, one boy would keep telling me that he had seen my house on fire and that all my family were dead, I believed him the first time, the second time I was more wary so he'd come up with new ways to convince me that this time they really were dead. I was probably about 8. I was picked on for saying or doing the wrong thing to someone and then their brothers and sisters would gang up on me and beat me up. I'd go home and my parents would tell me 'it's water off a duck's back' and I used to think, what does this have to do with ducks?? Or they would tell me I should have thicker skin, which also made no sense. I was bullied and harassed for years (often going home with torn clothes and no shoes, scratches and bruises) until one day, I fought back. A girl called Rebecca (who was a main ringleader) started punching me and for the first time, I thought to myself "hang on, I'm bigger than you I can hit you back" until then I was following the rules against violence and it had just never occurred to me to fight back, but I did and I won. It was a life changing moment for me, I realised I didn't have to be scared of bullies anymore and it changed me forever. I wonder now how things would have been different if the adults had just spoken to me in plain english and said "you can fight back" instead of confusing me with loads of idioms. For other children, fighting back would have been an instinctive response but I was trying to follow the rules.

At home, I liked to spend most of my time in the garden, collecting rocks and organising them or watching insects. I was obsessed with animals and anything to do with the natural world. In fact I was the only 7 year old in my class to answer "I want to be an entomologist when I grow up". I didn't mind some children but I found them confusing, so I would usually design the games we played and assign roles and responsibilities to people. I was more comfortable around adults and was often described as acting 'older than my age'. I used to think about things deeply and write poetry, I still remember one now "I am sleek, I am black, tears roll down back, sometimes down my sides as they hit the ground in tides". I had moments of clarity where maybe I was just sitting in the back of the car watching the world go by, and I felt like everyone is basically the same, we were all trying to eat, live, work -all on the same tiny planet. I could see that I was a person, in a town, in a country, on the planet, like everyone else. I was lucky that my parents let me have pets; we had a dog, a cat, a rabbit, a guinea pig, hamsters and mice over the years. I was always rescuing things if I found them injured, sometimes they would fare better after my intervention and sometimes (sorry to say ) worse. I was unintentionally clumsy and easily distracted. My room was always a mess, from having taken every game and book I owned out of its place or embarked on some project that then I was too attached to to dismantle (like mouse maze that spanned the whole room and stayed there for weeks).

However, I would cry about having my hair brushed, clothes that felt wrong, or having to have a bath or shower. I was an extremely fussy eater for tastes and textures and was very happy just eating the same thing every day if I could. I was considered a sensitive child. I watched TV shows about families like *The Cosby Show*, *The Waltons* and read comics at night, I learned a lot from these. I think I was looking for insight about values and behaviours and why people acted the way that they did. I taught myself to read Italian from the back of cereal boxes, when I stayed with my grandma and later french from reading french comics. I had an aptitude for languages and a complete ineptitude for maths (later diagnosed with dyscalculia).

Secondary school was a totally different story, around 13 I suddenly became 'pretty' and this made a lot of my weirdness forgivable and cool. I was also more confident generally, the new school had bullies but now I knew it was OK to stand up for myself. I started standing up for anyone who was being bullied and made friends with other 'weirdos'. I felt happy in their company, we would talk about whatever interests we had, go for walks and stuff like that. The popular crowd invited me to parties but also didn't really know what to do with me as I didn't fit the typical mould. On the outside I looked like a model but I acted like a weirdo, so it was a strange experience. I found watching people fascinating, how groups were formed and broken, how trends were picked up and dropped again. School didn't feel like the real world to me. I felt my interests were real and my close friends, but everything else just seemed like a pointless waste of energy. I was still a victim to naivety in relation to boys, puberty brought a whole range of new social rules that I had no idea about. I believed that if a boy wants to kiss you and says you're pretty then you're supposed to say yes. I lost all sense of self-autonomy in that respect. For example a boy telling me that I had to 'pleasure him' because he would have a stomach ache if I didn't. (Gross I know! And very stupid of me, but I was nice and I thought girls had to be nice all the time). Then I had a few horrible years that I don't want to go into here.

Eventually, I left school and home before finishing my studies. (I went back to them later). I had an amazing career, I didn't do anything in a 'straight line'. At 17 I volunteered in a Women's Centre, I got heavily into politics, I cared passionately about injustice and trying to make the world a better place. At 21 I did a course to learn more about multimedia and I trained to be web developer, which evolved into designing and building e-learning programs. This suited me so well, each new project was on a different subject and I realised I had a talent for absorbing lots of information quickly and I enjoyed then translating this into a way that others could understand. Wherever I worked I was promoted quickly, because I was passionate, responsible and focused. I didn't get sucked into office cliques and dramas, I just wanted to build the best learning experiences. I shaved all my hair off at one point because I was sick and tired of societal expectations about how I was supposed to be because I looked a certain way, and I didn't want attention from guys. My employers didn't mind that I wore a hat at my desk for the next few years because I couldn't bear the sensory feeling of having hair grow out and not being able to tie it back. I did well in my career often because there was one person who believed in me and let me do things 'my way'. Around 23 I went back to university part-time to study for a degree as I just felt I enjoyed learning, I was already in a career and I chose to do cultural studies. I did 5 years of a 6-year programme but then panicked at the idea of writing a thesis and quit (still annoyed at myself for doing that). However, my career was still going well by 35 I was working at a different company and I was the youngest senior executive, my ability to problem solve by seeing how things were connected across disciplines was valued, my employers appreciated that I could see the faults in the way they were doing things but that it wasn't personal to anyone, I just wanted to help the company to do better. My team liked that I was honest and focused on the outcome and that I let them work with autonomy and support too. Sadly at 38 I became seriously ill with Ehlers Danlos syndrome and had to give up work altogether. At this point, I'm looking for work that is flexible and that I can do from home.

I have consistent special interests and sporadic ones. The consistent ones are; culture and politics and the natural world. Sporadic ones tend to pop up depending on what's going on in my life, so as a child I decided that I didn't like the shape of the new London red buses, I liked the old kind with the open back you could jump onto and the spiral staircase. So I invented a project to make a petition. I knocked on every house in my neighbourhood and got people to sign it. But I didn't know what to do with it then, so the paper with signatures just sat in my bedroom for the next 10 years. My parents had no idea, until a neighbour said something about it. I'd just come up with these things and do them on my own. I decided I like birds at one point, so I gave myself an art project to draw all the different species of bird that live in wetlands. Other than that I mostly built habitats or games for my pets or for unfortunate wildlife that crossed my path.

I just felt like I didn't need other people, in the same way my friends and family did, people were 'out of sight out of mind'. I cared about them and felt sad or happy for them when things happened but it was like my own world was enriching and safe and I was the conductor of it.

As I got older, I found that the person I love easily becomes my special interest, they become the total focus of my attention. This is both wonderful and a slippery slide into codependency as I have discovered. So please be aware that this can be a tendency and if you have the wrong person it can be extremely detrimental to your self-esteem and identity. It's interesting because my son's psychologist told me that I am like a special interest to my son, in much the same way as dinosaurs or geography are to him, he would touch or bump into me constantly and need to be near me (not so much at home but when out and about). Yes he loves me, but I also perform functions for him that he needs. I'm like his personal pocket translator, trampoline and 'make-the-world-safe' maker. As an adult, I do the same to my partner - she translates what people say to me - I ask her "what did Bob mean by that?" Even though Bob is speaking English, I've no idea what he's talking about until she translates it into autistic for me. I use her like a trampoline (yes sex and firm hugs are extremely grounding for me), and I need her to simultaneously be my 'safe place' from the outside world and help shield me from it i.e. make excuses for why I don't go to functions. It's a lot of pressure to put on another person and too easy sometimes to use a relationship in this way. A little is harmless but a lot can be detrimental to both parties. Just something to bear in mind.

137

Quick pause just as I was writing this, as my partner called me to the garden to show me a strange insect (as she knows I love them!). I love special interests; they can create little beams of joy in an otherwise mundane day.

Moving on, for a while autism was definitely a special interest and I couldn't rest until I'd learned everything I could about it. It has been the same for all my health issues and often the health issues of people close to me. Most recently, reading and learning everything about Covid-19. Over the years I've been interested in photography, women's rights, class inequality, criminology, speech, language and communication disorders, self-sustainability and homesteading, diet and nutrition, specific animals, countries, languages, social media communities (how they form and grow), learning theory, psychology, law, gardening, films, writing, journalism and probably loads more that I can't remember right now.

It's a bit like with music, sometimes I hear a song and I just love it and have to play it over and over again until suddenly I've had enough of it. It's like that with interests, I don't know what will grab my attention and curiosity 3 months from now, but when it happens it's exciting and immersive. It becomes a way that I simultaneously relax and exercise my brain at the same time. It's extremely important to me to be learning something new all the time. The only times in my life when I haven't done this are when I have been depressed, which of course made the depression worse and more dangerous.

I am unemployed due to health issues. It is funny that my skills and experience are so varied that writing a CV is always a mammoth task as I have to leave things out depending on the job, as people would find it improbable that I had done so many things and that I could be any good at doing them all. I'm currently looking for work that's flexible; I can do translation between French, Italian, Spanish and English. I can write articles, graphic design, build websites, build learning programmes. Pretty much you could give me any subject and I could come up with a 10-point presentation that would inspire and amaze you. So you'd think I'd have a job of some kind, but I'm currently paralysed with anxiety about committing to anything. My health issues mean that I'd have to bail and let people down if I suddenly had an issue, which makes me very uncomfortable as I like to be dependable. So it's just something I'm working on overcoming at the moment.

## How and when did you make the connection between you and autism?

As a young adult I just thought I was a bit different but I didn't obsess over it, I had already left home and picked my own friends (who were all unique like me one way or another), these were people I could have deep conversations with and who didn't take offence if I didn't talk to them for months at a time. I was diagnosed with dyspraxia, dyscalculia and dyslexia at university and I attributed most of my 'out of the box' style and thinking to those conditions. Romantically, I now know I had a typical problem that a lot of autistic people have which is not understanding the rules of love and thus allowing other people to dictate them for us. I was naive and kind, and desperate to try and create a settled family unit of my own. I met someone when I was 21, we fell in love quickly. She seemed confident and knowledgeable about how relationships were supposed to be, so I didn't question it when I'd say I had to travel somewhere far for work and she'd insist I travel back the same day (even if it was a 5am - 2am day). She told me that 'Love is never wanting to be apart from someone else, not even for one night'. 'Love is not keeping any secrets and sharing everything together' so I didn't question it when she insisted that I didn't see my friends alone or that she wanted to read all my emails and text messages. 'Love is caring about each other' so I didn't question it when she said that all the furniture had to be in her taste and the big decisions had to be her decisions, because she said that showed I cared. Blah blah blah. She would put me down constantly and make fun of me, I took it because I had this default switch in my brain that said "you have no idea what you're doing, you're on an alien planet and you need a guide". My default was that whatever the situation it was probably me who was in the wrong. All my life people had pointed out things that were a bit odd or different so it was logical to come to that conclusion. Unsurprisingly of course, being with a bad partner, diminishes you and they start lamenting "Why can't you be happy like you were before".

We had a son when I was 29, and after that her jealousy and possessive behaviour intensified. It was because I loved him in a pure way that I could see how toxic our relationship had become and that I didn't want him to grow up surrounded by that. So I divorced her when he was about 2.5years old. Then I met someone new a little while later, who loved (as she put it) that 'I marched to the beat of my own drum'. By then Jack was about 4 years old. He had started 'stimming' and showing an obsessive interest in dinosaurs and little interest in other children. It was my new partner who suggested that maybe there was something wrong with him. I thought he was completely 'normal'. I had been the same after all. I was worried that maybe he was traumatised from the divorce and that it would be a good idea to have him checked out by a child psychologist. That's when he was diagnosed and I learnt so much about autism.

First of all, I assumed that it was perfectly normal to have to explain everything to a child, how would they know anything otherwise? But I was informed that kids are just supposed to 'pick up' on all the implied social rules without them being explained (like when and how to say thank you, how to join a game that others are playing etc). It was fascinating, I had been working on my own mental "Handbook for how to be a human" all my life. If it had been a real book it would have been well-worn, with lots of notes in the margins as it got updated from new experiences and there would have been chapters for every social situation you can imagine. I thought being a parent was all about passing down this virtual book. Turns out, other people just don't need it. Who knew??

So now we had a diagnosis and at first I was really upset and worried for Jack, but after a few days of processing the diagnosis it dawned on me, that if I had all the same traits and I turned out OK, that it wasn't some kind of sad death-sentence-of-a-diagnosis, but actually just a helpful thing to know so I could help him relate to the world and the world relate back to him. I understood him, I knew why he needed to stim, why he couldn't tie his shoelaces but could recite the names of 200 dinosaurs.

What I found really strange, was how other people processed his diagnosis, I thought my friends and family would feel better, the reason he wasn't so sociable wasn't because they were doing something wrong, so why take it personally? I flipped my mental virtual handbook from NT to autistic and basically said "look this is a handbook for how to relate to an autistic person" and I tried to pass on my wisdom of everything I'd learned about autism (drawing also on my own experiences) for how a neurotypical person should relate to an autistic person to be able to understand each other. But wow. People were not flexible, they didn't want to have to learn how to talk to him; I'd say "don't ask him questions that put him on the spot" and "talk to him about dinosaurs". But honestly, they just didn't understand, and I think it's because they had the privilege their whole lives of people adapting to their way of thinking, that it just seemed too alien and too much effort to make their own words and actions conscious. So I watched them make the same mistakes over and over again with him. It was painful.

My son had to learn to say hello and goodbye to people, why wasn't this automatic? It's obvious, if I see you and you see me, why do we need words to underline an already obvious fact? Why do his teachers ask him questions they already know the answer to? Of course as an adult I know why, but I also know these things need to be explained to him and I don't assume that he is somehow supposed to know automatically. So whenever he deals with NTs he is supposed to hold in his head a list of 25 things he needs to do to make the other people present feel comfortable, but they can't reciprocate and do the same for him. In reality, as my son grows up he has been able to adapt to them better than the other way around. Grr. Right! Now because I'm cross, I'm actually going to write out 25 things that we're expected to do upon walking into a room, let's imagine walking into a room where there are two parents and three of their friends.

1. Enter room, but don't jerk the door handle loudly, or swing the door open too hard.
2. Look at everyone in the room.
3. Say 'hello' to each person (but vary between 'Hello', 'Hi', 'Hi ya' or you'll make it weird).
4. Depending on the type of relationship you have with the people and how long since you last saw them, choose an option that reflects that "how are you?", "how's it going" (as above vary it).
5. Depending on their culture, give each person a kiss or a hug, or a hug AND a kiss, or a hi-five, man half-hug/shoulder bump, or a handshake. Do not do all these things at once.
6. Remember their names.
7. Decide where to sit so you can face them (not in the corner).

8. Ignore any lights, smells or sounds that are distracting you.

9. Listen to what people say and wait the appropriate amount of time to respond.

10. Respond in a way that shows you were listening (this varies between cultures).

11. Don't interrupt even if you have something interesting to say and you will forget it in 0.5 seconds.

12. When each person asks you "How's school" answer it as if it is the first time you have heard it.

13. Choose 3 things from the 500 things that happened at school and tell each person.

14. When they say "that used to be my favourite subject" and proceed to tell you wrong information about that subject, DO NOT correct them. This will embarrass them or start an argument.

15. Have you given eye contact yet?

16. If someone offers you something, you must take it and consume it, even if it makes your skin crawl.

17. They will start talking to each other about things you don't know or care about. You must stay where you are and nod.

18. Do not introduce a new subject of conversation they don't understand or care about, that is rude.

19. Do not look at the clock, this will be interpreted as rude.

20. Do not look at your shoes, this will be interpreted as rude.

21. Do not fidget, this will be interpreted as rude.

22. You have no idea when you are allowed to leave, you must wait patiently until someone else leaves,

or make up an excuse that will not be interpreted as rude. Any excuse can be interpreted as rude.

23. When you leave, say "goodbye" to each person, but also say "bye", "bye, nice to see you", "take care" if you say the same thing 4 times it will be seen as weird.
24. Hug, kiss or wave goodbye, depending on the culture of the other people and how well you know them. You don't know their culture, so take a guess. Getting it wrong will be perceived as rude.
25. Don't accidentally slam the door on the way out.

To this day, I find it ludicrous that NT people think that we're the ones that aren't adaptable!! Which reminds me, 5 years ago, while I was sat there staring at my son's extremely negative and depressing autism assessment report. I had started to worry about how autism would affect my son as he grew up, it sounded so 'definite', a list of all the things that were different and difficult for him, how would he cope? He was only 4.5 years old. Then as I realised I was autistic, it put it into perspective, yes I was an odd child who grew up to be an odd adult, BUT I managed to have a great career, interests, family and friends, I didn't need to be 'written off' at 5 years old and neither would my son. I didn't have the benefit of insight and awareness about autism to help me on my path but he would.

The NT world seems to forget that we're humans, we're not 'totally fixed' a particular way forever from birth. We can learn. Let me repeat that, we can learn for ourselves. I know it seems obvious but people genuinely forget that and dismiss the whole person or they treat autistic people like animals and try and 'train' children into their way of thinking and acting.

You may have heard about 'masking'. Masking is basically the process of using your experience and logic to determine how to act in given situations. Some aspects of 'masking' become automatic, and some don't. The key thing about learning how to 'adapt' is that it should be a partnership between the adult and the child, what does the child want to be able to do and how to help them do it, whilst valuing their authentic selves at all times.

The problem with having to mask is that it's really tiring and often feels degrading (I have to act this way to appear as the same value as you and your needs always come before mine). I think NTs mask too sometimes, but although that makes this concept relatable for them, it's not quite the same. For an autistic person the process of learning to mask is a survival technique and sadly our guides were often misguided and forced us to mask to do things that really don't matter (the 25 point list above becomes 100 things depending how much the NT people around the autistic person value conformity).

Parents, teachers and other role models and other guides who are preoccupied with 'what other people think' don't realise how many times they prioritise the vague expectations of strangers over the core well-being of the autistic person they profess to love. This can be extremely harmful and can cause depression, general anxiety such as ongoing mental paralysis over tiny decisions.

It takes a long time to undo poor coping mechanisms once they've been created. I'm still extremely sensitive to criticism because I feel I try so hard all the time to fit in, not offend or not embarrass myself. Somewhere along the line, I've picked up the message that I'm only acceptable as a person if I am acceptable to other people. So that now criticisms/sarcasm/banter aimed at me just cut right through me and I feel immediately anxious and unsure of what the repercussions will be. I'm made aware that I've transgressed in some way, but because the rules are so complex and my experiences so negative, I've no idea what that means in Neurotypical-Land. "Will I be beheaded, ostracised or ridiculed? Maybe I'll have to walk a plank?" I get told it was "just a joke"? Or that 'they didn't mean anything by it'. But why say something you didn't mean? And how do I know that at the time? And can I trust they are telling me the truth now, if they didn't mean what they said then? It's foreign to me.

I think often when people (young people and adults) realise that they're autistic then it's natural to go through an intense process of trying to unburden themselves of all aspects of masking/coping they can now reject, they start to figure out 'what is truly me' versus 'what is the me when I am around you' (other NTs). They can start to forgive themselves for past failures where they felt they didn't fit in, and learn to love themselves just as they are according to their own standards.

Some people can mask extremely well, others hardly at all. I really do feel that it's like being a foreigner, you might speak the language but you still have an 'accent' and make the occasional slip that gives you away. I still find it excruciating when that happens, I think "oh this interaction is going well" and then I say or do something that makes me want to slap myself. The process of self-acceptance is definitely ongoing! Which is also why it's vital to have neurodiverse friends who 'get it' and will laugh 'with you' and not 'at you' at times like that.

I think my son is very lucky to have an autistic parent, because I'm able to understand his reactions and motivations in a way that others can't. Being autistic (I think) also helps me to recognise what is really important. For example, does it matter if he behaves in an 'obviously' autistic way? I don't try and make him suppress his stims, but I've seen other parents try to do so, in order to make it 'the autism' look less obvious. They seem to genuinely believe that they are helping their kids to 'fit in' but actually it just shows that the parent is ashamed and cares more about total strangers than the fact that the person needs to regulate their own nervous system so they can cope in that moment. The list goes on; does it really matter if a kid eats chips with their fingers? Does it matter if he doesn't have tons of friends as long as he has a few good ones? Do they have to eat different food? Wear different clothes? etc etc

I know I was very lucky to have him and if I could, I'd have five more just like him. We have in depth conversations about whatever his interests are and I respect them and his autonomy. I feel like we have built a strong trusting bond because I didn't try and mould him into what I thought he should be, I just see my job as helping him to discover and appreciate himself whilst also navigating the NT world. Our children are growing up in a world where through the power of the internet, they will be able to find kindred spirits and hopefully they won't have to struggle the same way we did. Of course there are other dangers and concerns about the world that we didn't have, but at least with support of a broader community hopefully these can be handled together.

He is now almost 11 and doing great, I carried on explaining everything to him and it's worked out well for us. I've learned that I'm sensory-avoidant and he is sensory-seeking (which has been hard on us at times). Through the diagnosis we have found a language that we both understand. He knows that when I need time to decompress that it's nothing he has done wrong, I know that when he says he doesn't want to eat something (i.e. being a 'fussy eater') that he can't help it and eventually like me he'll be able to enjoy a wider variety of foods - he already eats way more than he used to. We know what is important - whatever interest we have at the moment, support and having fun.

**Did you seek an official assessment?**
I am self-realised, I considered pursuing it at the time that my son was diagnosed but I didn't have the money to do it then, so I joined some online support groups for autistic women and found that they gave me so much helpful information that I haven't felt I really needed to get officially diagnosed. I've made lifelong friends

through those groups and we understand each other. It's awesome. I'm also diagnosed with dyslexia, dyspraxia, Irlen's syndrome (visual issues), auditory processing difficulties, migraines so in the past I've used those when I have needed accommodations at work. For my son I could see the many ways that having a formal diagnosis could help him be understood at school and it will help him understand himself better as he grows up. Having the label for when he needs it, also means he can seek out social groups and peer support when he's older. He also has the choice to withhold the diagnosis from employers or friends as he wishes. For me, now that I'm an adult I don't see the benefit, it won't help me get accommodations or change my life in any tangible way. If someone were to offer me the chance at an assessment for free, I'd take it. But otherwise I'm living with various chronic illnesses due to Ehlers Danlos syndrome, that I can't face going down another diagnosis path. So maybe someday I will, but for now, my closest friends and family accept me for who I am. People know that a room can't be too bright, that certain sounds are unbearable to me, they accept that I always wear black leggings, a long-sleeved black top and flowy light dress over it all (as anything else would rub and squeeze my skin and I wouldn't be able to concentrate). They know I get tired quickly from social situations and that I don't often go to functions, not because I don't like the people there (well sometimes that's why). But mostly it's because people want to talk 'small talk', which to me is just 1000 ways to say the wrong thing and is very tedious and repetitive.

I also don't drink, not because I'm morally opposed to it, I just don't like to drink or get hangovers. It means that the little I understood of what people were saying to me before they started drinking goes out the window. I also have real problems understanding what people are saying to me, I can hear the person next to me but also every other person in the room at the same time. I find myself staring at their mouths trying to lip read but that doesn't help. Then add to that, the high probability that the owners of the venue or home have opted for the latest trendy fashion of having spotlights, bare lightbulbs or see-through lampshades (you know the kind, where you can see the filament) and it's like trying to talk to someone with sun in your eyes, whilst two different people are talking into each ear. So nope, not a fun experience and then finally if I've attended the party with an NT person, it's guaranteed that I'll get comments afterwards like "Why did you say that?", or "Why didn't you say that" and I have to go through the shame of feeling like I offended people.

I really need the right balance of personal time vs social time 70%/30% or I get worn out and irritable. My partner and close friends are mostly understanding when I say the wrong thing or say the right thing but at the wrong time but it's still an ongoing joke that I don't seem to know how to say goodbye on the phone properly (surely you just say goodbye?). Still no idea. But that's OK, no one is good at everything.

The irony is that, having experienced what they were like when my son was diagnosed, it made me realise that a label for me would make no difference. They still wouldn't understand, it's easier for them to just understand "This is Dom and Dom likes X and doesn't like Y". Unofficially though they make comments like "you're being autistic again" when I say something doesn't make sense or take something literally. It is much harder to mask as you get older, I think my sensory issues are much worse than they used to be, and I don't have the energy or inclination to try and fit in anymore. I think acquaintances just think I'm a bit odd but harmless. I'm either extremely quiet or insanely talkative and hyper, the latter if I like someone.

I see people really struggling about whether to get diagnosed or not, and if they do get a diagnosis then they seem to (incorrectly) believe that a cascade of understanding and adaptations will come their way. If they don't get assessed then they seem plagued with self-doubt, especially if they are not living in an 'autistic friendly' environment where all the people around them are giving them horrible opinions about what they think is wrong with them. Ultimately, I'm satisfied enough that I'm autistic and having this knowledge has helped me to understand myself and develop more resilience to other people's opinions of me and my needs. If I was still living with my parents or around negative people, then maybe getting an official diagnosis would give me peace of mind and allow me to shut them out.

**Are you aut?**
I don't generally tell people who I don't know because they don't understand what it is, so mostly it would be like saying to someone "Hi I'm a snoozerflowt" except if

anything, instead of inspiring a helpful question back to you like "Oh what's a snoozerflowt?" they now understand you less, because the word 'Autism' has so many stereotypes that are wrong and stupid that even mentioning makes a lot of people treat you even more alien than they did before. They don't ask "what is autistic?" they say "Oh I've heard of that" and then the next things they say are completely wrong and instead of having an interesting conversation, you find yourself explaining and defending yourself and it's just a horrible process. "No, I'm not good at maths", "Yes girls present differently", "No, I'm not like your 5 year old nephew", "No, I'm not just making this up for attention", "No, I don't look autistic", "No they don't have a cure", "No, I don't want a cure", "No, I don't need your sympathy", "No, it's not because of mobile phone radiation/not enough vegetables/because it's fashionable", "No, I don't like trains" etc etc it goes on and on. Those people that have been officially diagnosed, seem to get the same treatment with an added eye roll to indicate they assume you were diagnosed by a quack.

I do educate and inform people if it comes up in conversation but I find this much easier to do if they don't know I'm autistic, it feels less personal. I might casually mention that I think I'm autistic depending on how positively they respond. It's also relevant that because I'm gay, and have a chronic illness that means I use a cane. I have to worry about whether to 'Come Out' with every interaction and honestly I don't have the energy or enthusiasm to spend all day explaining how I'm a lesbian (even though I don't 'look' like one) and why I'm autistic (even though I don't look like it) and why I use a cane (even though I'm young). We really don't owe anyone an explanation.

**What are your thoughts about the autistic characters in TV series and movies?**

I've watched *the Good Doctor, Big Bang Theory* and *Rain Man*. The latter was so long ago now, that I don't think the autistic community need to worry about the harmful stereotypes perpetuated by Dustin Hoffman. My thoughts on popular TV culture that has autistic characters is that, sometimes they help and sometimes they hinder. Take the *Big Bang Theory* - (the writers by the way have never acknowledged that Sheldon is autistic) on the one hand the character is full of stereotypes - socially awkward, male, genius, selfish, asexual etc that is annoying for most autistic people who aren't like that. On the other hand, it shows people who would otherwise believe that autistic people should only be in an institution, that we can live full lives with friends and a career. On a personal note, I think it's a very funny programme. *The Good Doctor* was pretty good, Shawn felt true to his character, but again not representative of every autistic person. In summary I think there just needs to be more characters and diversity of characters in popular TV shows. It would be nice to see some female autistic characters that I actually recognise!

**What would you like to say to someone wondering if they might be autistic?**

Realising you're autistic and learning to accept it as an important part of you is a process. There are times where you will hate the autistic parts of yourself, it will feel like something that gets in the way of everything you want to do. I hope that you will get to the point that I have, where, I really value the aspects of my autistic self and I've surrounded myself with people who I genuinely like. I think we are gifted with a radar for bullshit and 'bad' people (especially once we learn that people should be judged by their actions and not what they say) so many social norms are made up and so much of what people say isn't what they mean. What is OK in one country is awful in another country. Being autistic is like realising you're from another country with different customs and that's completely OK. It's not fair to be made to feel like you're wrong for doing things differently. Funnily enough, the most empathetic, non-judgmental and nice people I've met have been autistic, they should be more like us. So if you haven't reached out to some autistic and neurodiverse communities before, do it now.

# Gender, romantic and sexual life

•

- "I'm female and call myself female or say my sex and gender is. But I have no real connection to it, frankly. I see myself as a person. I don't really feel comfortable with the non-binary label personally, though I respect when others call themselves that and want to be addressed as such.
I'm LGBTQI+. I'm pansexual but have only had relationships with men. I wouldn't mind being in a relationship with a woman or with a transgendered person. I'm not looking for a relationship and don't know if I ever will again though. It may be the medication I'm on (SSRI's etc) or just the trauma from the last relationship."


- "I was born as a female, and I always had intimate and sexual relationships only with males.
But I feel I am not REALLY gendered, I think of myself as a person. Or maybe as a child."


- "Personally, I relate to the female gender."


- "I believe I am female, simply because of the parts that I have. While there may be tendencies and stereotypes with men and women, I don't believe you have to fit any of those to be your assigned gender. I am heterosexual.

157

I understand that many have different views than me on this, and that is valid as well. We're all humans, worthy of love and respect :)"


- "I identify as Female. I think of myself as queer, but I prefer not to get any more specific than that."


- "I am a bi-romantic, straight demigirl. First I thought I was just bisexual (from the age of 6), but later I read stuff about gender and sexuality in online forums and recognised myself in this description.
I am single for four years now, but I am kind of romantic and hope to marry a kind, patient, handsome guy one day."


- " I am feminine, the world of sewing allowed me to be more feminine and become the woman that I am, but honestly, I feel like I'm a 'thing' which does not really know if it exists or not. Sometimes yes, I take on the feminist activist side, with the fragility that this entails, and being a woman forces us to assume everything alone for years, yes, these struggles of women in society speak to me. I can choose to wear makeup or not (my "war paintings", as I say), I can dress for the occasion or not, based on how I feel that day. But if I could compare myself to a thing or to a person, I would prefer to compare myself to a cat. I have this way of loving to socialize on certain occasions (however my family are ultra-sociable and even a bit clingy at times), but I love my independence and when people push me too much I claw and hiss! Kssssss! Hihh.

I don't know, in regards to gender whether I'm more masculine or feminine, what is being feminine or masculine? It's what society tells us to be. I like to wear makeup but just like certain Indian, African and other tribes, I also have my war paint, but I wear it according to the current social code in fashion. I know how to appreciate my feminine side, I learned this from my close friends who were like sisters and true guides. In terms of romance, I don't think I am very romantic. I'm more realistic in my expectations, 'I want this', 'I want that', 'don't do this to me', 'don't do that to me', that's more what I'm like. In fact, when it comes to romance contours and forms, I am often laughing when I see that I missed the moment and that the other person had expected a little romanticism from me.
But it's good that (surprisingly) they don't blame me for that, rather we laugh about it together. I don't position myself clearly as a woman or man, neither in my thoughts, nor in my feelings, although my man tells me that I am an extra-terrestrial, that it makes sense that I am not typically female, because he tells me that I don't drive like a woman, and the same in the way that I react to things, I think he has never seen someone like me and he feels close to me because he also has a way of being that's atypical of most men, and so when it comes to the feminine or masculine parts in each of us, we don't really think about it.

I actually think that I got through life without really wondering about these issues, it's like I was in a form of denial of myself, or of the shape I have had since birth. I have pictures of me where I am told that I seem to be elsewhere, that I rarely look comfortable. Photos of me are scarce, often I don't even recognize myself, it's like the difference between the person I see in the mirror and the one I see in the photo is so big that I tell myself that it doesn't look like me.

Strangely, even my man says so. He does not recognize me and it's as if I were another, or that I become another that he does not know while someone takes my picture. Therefore, there is obviously a gap between our outside and our inside. However, I have no sexual ambiguity in my sexual preferences (100% hetero). I already tried with a childhood girl friend when we were teenagers, but more because she suggested it to me and thought 'why not try?' but nope, I felt disgust and it did not make me want to try it again. I can appreciate something aesthetically beautiful. I like to look at beautiful women, sometimes it's just a detail, I can look at women the same as I would look at a man, but I think it's more aesthetics than anything else, I could not see myself with a woman even if I thought she was superb. I like beautiful energies too, whether it is a woman or a man, I like spending time with a person whose energy is positive, even if I have to take a long time to recover afterwards, but it does me good. I am wholehearted in my relationships. That's why I need to have a very small circle and not have too many people in my life. But if I know people well, I'm happy to meet up with them and even if in the long term we don't get along, or in the sense of being friends, it's ok because we don't necessarily have to be stuck together all the time. It's not always easy to get along with everyone, but I can appreciate a person and not need to meet or see them very often.

The idea of emotional and sexual orientation being two separate dimensions makes sense to me because I can indeed have times when I feel more emotionally attracted to men or women, depending on who I meet. I once had a very good relationship with two men, I really wanted to be with them so much that I even thought I was in love but in fact, no it was just our laughs, our discussions on various subjects, their way of seeing life, I liked their presence, I felt like I was wrapped in cotton. But as soon as we had to clarify our relationship, it was difficult, I felt trapped and it was hard for me to tell them what I really felt for them because for me it was clear that there would never be anything more (I did even try to start a relationship with one of them, the other physically repelled me, I couldn't even kiss him on the cheek), but they wanted me to define our relationship. Firstly because they had other women in their lives, it was already complicated enough for them to have this relationship with me without having to explain why we called each other so often and that we just loved spending time together, even just walking around laughing and talking nonsense.

Another example, I have an ex who I was with for 5 years who wouldn't define himself and often compared himself to David Bowie who he was a fan of. He had a side that was not typical of his gender, he dressed any way he liked with what he was given and what he found, he didn't buy clothes. Sometimes it would produce improbable outfits, I laughed with him. We separated but continued to live our friendship without sexual hindrance because he didn't like it too much and I hate sweating and excessively acidic skin anyway. I have a hard time with certain skin smells and textures, maybe that's also why I cannot be with a woman, I would feel like I was making love to myself and as I have no feeling or pleasure in touching myself, I don't know maybe it's something like that. Anyway, I also had female friends like these two friends with whom I liked to share a certain degree of intimacy, without touching each other of course, we were like sisters, but I liked their presence and they felt close to me. They reassured me and also mentally stimulated me. So, I have had very strong emotional relationships with men and women, but only sexually attracted to men and a good man in this case. I like his 'bear' side, it's super sexy. LOL

Everyone is free to live their life as they see fit and as well as they can with what was given to them at birth and if nature has got things wrong, well this person can become what they need to be, why not. I have no particular judgment or opinion. People are free, as long as no one comes to tell me how I should live, I don't care. »


- « I identify as she/her, but I do not feel a connection to a particular gender. Personally, I am OK with people labeling me as cis, for the simple reason that I don't want to explain the very complicated way I define my identity. For most of my life I thought I was straight, but I learned about asexuality and demi-sexuality a couple years ago and I believe that I'm actually somewhere on that spectrum. I am still figuring myself out like I think a lot of us are, and I've found a wonderful queer community in my area that's just as supportive as the one I've found with other autistics. I believe everyone should question gender and sexuality once in a while... it doesn't have to change how you see yourself, but I think it's healthy.

My thoughts on gender are pretty complicated, I guess. I think I understand why autistics tend to have a higher amount of trans/non-binary people among us than in the neurotypical population, and to me it's obvious. Since gender is largely a performative social construct, and people on the spectrum live in a world where social norms and rules never made sense to them in the first place, it's only natural for us to question gender norms."


- "It is a social construct, a role assignment a majority of people seem to just take on without questioning... I always felt bewildered by it. It was one of my biggest difference factors in relation to peers as a child, I didn't mention it in the other question because it had more to do with my gender and sexual identity than my autism, but I didn't fit in with the girls with what they were doing and how they were talking among themselves, and I also didn't fit in with the boys although they were easier to play with sometimes... but because I was physically a girl they wouldn't let me and ridiculed me when they found out I liked girls.

So I started questioning what it meant to be one or the other gender, and found that I find the concept ridiculous, that based on the physical sex, you can only do this or that and not other things. I find it a concept that needs to be overthrown so that people can be seen for who they individually are instead of pushing them into roles.

My sex is female. I have a lot of things in my life experience that are inherently tied to that and make me relate to being a woman. Other things of being a woman I can't relate to at all, so I would say I am a gender-non-conforming female, but its rather a decision from excluding other possibilities that I relate to even less. I heard of the concept of "autigender", now that is something I could fully accept for me, but I don't think it's that established. I'd be "autigender female" or something like that.

I am a lesbian."


- "I am female and I am straight.
Although I believe love is love and if you meet the right person then nothing should stop you being with them.
I completely support the LGBTQI+ spectrum and have many friends who are on it.
I believe as long as you aren't hurting anyone you should feel free to express yourself and love however you feel."


- "I'm a cisgender, heterosexual woman. I don't know much about the gender spectrum. I don't see why people get upset when someone comes out as transgender though – if someone identifies as a different gender to the one they were assigned with at birth, it doesn't harm anyone else. People should be encouraged to be themselves and embrace their own identities. Life's too short to spend it trying to be someone else.

A bit unrelated to the question, but I suppose that's one thing I also struggle to understand. Racism, sexism, homophobia, transphobia etc – we're all just people and these characteristics logically do not determine our abilities or character. To me it seems absurd that some people seem to think otherwise, although I guess some people are more susceptible to developing unconscious biases than others."


- "I don't know anymore [about gender]. That's it. LOL I would normally answer I identify as female, but I don't know anymore. I guess I pend more to agender these days, but it has no impact on my life other than me reflecting a lot about it. I use female pronouns and identify with them.

I'm a lesbian. I think it is a big part of who I am and why I normally think of myself as a female. I am always questioning everything, tho... That includes my sexuality, my gender, my career, my study field. But I definitely am on the LGBTQI+ spectrum".


- "Gender is interesting, I identify as female, however I do from time to time have male tendencies and traits, so I would consider myself a tomboy, a term used for ages but I know some people are not happy with that terminology. I am also bisexual and demisexual as well, which means I have to create a strong emotional bond with someone before anything can be taken further, I'm also open to poly and open relationships, although at the moment I am in a monogamous relationship with a guy."


- "I don't fully grasp the concept of gender, more precisely what it seems to mean for the rest of the population.
I am biologically a woman, and I have no problem with that. I inhabit my female body and I feel comfortable in it. I actually like this body, it's not perfect but I never had any complex. I even enjoyed having my periods, the whole woman/moon cycle thing. I truly feel biologically a woman.
However I don't relate to the woman experience. I don't share the interests, activities and life events usually associated with being a woman. I never cared much about getting married, being the Princess of the Day in a white gown, I never was into make-up, jewels, clothes, fashion, home decoration, being in a relationship, having the whole "adult woman" status. I don't dislike any of those, I do use undereye concealer and decorate my home, they just don't ring any special bell in me. I tremendously dislike chitchatting over the phone for hours. A phone conversation has to last maximum 10 minutes and be useful and productive. Like at what time do we meet, or what's the plan for Christmas.

Nevertheless there's a lot of femininity in me, I'm sensitive, feminine looking, refined and graceful. In parallel there's also a lot of masculinity. I live my life and often react, think and behave like men do (as per the general mainstream sense).

Yet I can't say I am bi-gender, or a-gender. It doesn't reflect either how I feel. Those terms are too clear-cut, too dual. What I feel is both female and male in a "yin-yang" way: all mixed together.

After much thinking and researching and interacting in the queer community, the best way I found to describe my feeling about my gender and gender in general, is that gender is not an attribute. It's a full identity, it is core, and it is made of 3 intertwined dimensions: biological, energetical and social construction.

Traditional Chinese Medicine states that females' vital energy is 2/3 yin and 1/3 yang, and males' energy is 2/3 yang and 1/3 yin. I believe that concept is true, but some of us human beings have different ratios. It's actually a spectrum. Gender is a spectrum, as well as sexuality. I feel I am made of yin and yang in a balanced way ("50-50"), and like the Yin-Yang symbol one stems from the other and they form a whole.

So, in a nutshell, my gender is biologically female, energetically both equally female and male merged into one energy and I don't relate to the social construct part of genders."

- "I'm fine with my gender, I did have some confusion as a kid because someone told me that lesbians are females who wished they were men, and because that didn't apply to me, it delayed me realising I was a lesbian. I'm not an expert in this area, I just know that

I fully support people's right to determine all the elements of their identity.

I would like to say that having had an autistic boy and autistic brother I feel like there are big differences. Boys tend to be more competitive, attracted to mechanical machines like trains and cars, less aware or interested in the social differences they might have compared to their peers, people are more forgiving of their introversion. The autistic women I've met, have had to cope as girls, with a lot more societal pressure to be considerate of others at all times, and to dress and behave in a way that is considered feminine. I wholly reject the idea of autism being an 'extreme male brain', that's codswallop. Ultimately I hope the assessment process 'gets with the times' and stops looking for male traits before they consider autism as a valid diagnosis. Thankfully there are plenty of women in social media to provide role models.

For autistic boys I really worry for them as they grow up. One of my latest special interests is incel subculture (don't look it up unless you're mentally prepared), but basically it seems to me that many of these young men are being harmed. They believe the reason they can't form a relationship with young women is because they are somehow flawed from birth (genetically inferior) and that women are shallow, and only use sex to get material things/perpetuate a strong gene pool. Trust me, there's a lot more to it than that, but that's the gist.

I worked for a while in the criminal justice system, one of the programmes we had was working with sexual offenders who were male and diagnosed with Asperger's. They were imprisoned for offences such as following girls home, not knowing when advances had been rejected and why, not understanding how to recognise what was sexually appropriate or inappropriate behaviour. They seemed to have had no supportive male role models to 'show them the way' of how to be around women. Macho culture and sexism in pornograpy had utterly reinforced negative stereotypes about how women like to be treated and confused them. I really believe that as a community we must not let the boys get 'left behind', we need to encourage them to support each other and build friendships with women based on mutual interests.

The incel culture is full of awful 'motivational speakers' who target young (mostly 13-21 year old), lonely men with poor social skills and simply reinforce negative ideas that ultimately lead to depression and sometimes suicide of these young men. And sadly, serious harm of women and girls who are treated badly by them along the way.

Of course, autistic women suffer greatly when it comes to societal sexism, I would guess that the rate of sexual abuse against autistic women is probably as high as 9 in every 10 autistic women have been sexually, physically or emotionally abused. My hope is that even as we move forward recognising that gender stereotypes don't have to play a major part in our identities, that we also root out and deal with the problems that plague men and women in cultures where it is not OK to have traits of the other and respect each other as possibly different but equal."


- "In regard to romantic attraction, I have been bi-romantic all my life, but I have only dated men. My friendships with women have always been very intense and consuming, I didn't realize until recently they were not the mainstream definition of friendship. Actually, friendship and love are on a spectrum as well, and friendship is one of the many forms of love. I don't understand why as soon as sex is involved the related love is considered differently, like it's another dimension. It's not. Love is love and all forms co-exist on a spectrum, with or without sexuality.
Now since a couple of years I am 100% homo-romantic, I feel romantic attraction only for women.

My sexuality has changed as well over time. All my life I have been demi-sexual, i.e. I felt sexual attraction only when forming a strong romantic bond with someone. When not in a relationship I never felt sexual attraction. It's pretty cool because I never felt frustration in between relationships. Now I am asexual: I don't feel any sexual attraction for anyone. I did love sex. I'm just not attracted anymore. It's not a choice, yet I'm really fine with it. It's very appeasing."

# Synesthesia

The autistic wiring of the brains leads to sensorial hyper- (or hypo-) sensitivity. But not only: synesthesia is another phenomenon that is commonly experienced by Auties.

Synesthesia is a neurological trait or condition that results in a joining or merging of senses (or cognitive pathways) that aren't normally connected. The stimulation of one sense causes an involuntary reaction in one or more of the other senses (or cognitive paths). For example, someone with synesthesia may hear colors or see sounds.

It's wild. I love it. It plays a huge role in creativity, for instance.

•

- "I see choreographies while listening to music."

- "I see the days and months on a 3D spiral."

- "I see days of the week in colors:
monday = indian, muted pink
tuesday = plum
wednesday = teal
thursday = mustard yellow
friday = nut brown
saturday = very dark green
sunday = pearl grey"

- "My [autistic] son has assigned a color to each of the family members. He gave me yellow."

- "Monday - Greenish.
Tuesday - Blueish on the light side.
Wednesday - Some light orangey/lilac color mixed.
Thursday - Dark blue.
Friday – Purpleish.
Saturday and Sunday - light beige/brown mixed, Sunday slightly darker color than Saturday.

I also view individual letters in colors. Same with months also."

- "Monday is light tan, Tuesday is dark blue, Wednesday is medium slate, Thursday is blackish blue, Friday is rust-colored, Saturday is white, and Sunday is black. Each day has a different shape, too."

- "I'm a music-color synesthete. I am also a feel-to-color synesthete. A great book about synesthesia is called Tasting the Rainbow by Maureen Seaberg. Check it out!"

- "I have sound synesthesia. I see sounds."

- "I have chromesthesia: musical instruments (the timbres), musical pitches, and voices, plus other sounds, make colors for me.
Some other synesthetic connections, too, like calendars in space and colored letters, but the colorful music is my main one."

- "I see colors and shapes when I hear sounds."

- "I taste music, well some music/certain sounds. Like viola always tastes like cedar wood smoke but some music groups have no taste at all."

- "I only had that happen to me once. I saw colors and felt the wind on my skin and a taste of fresh water in my mouth. I was listening to Frank Bridge's piano quartet, Phantasy. I was in a concert hall. It was magical!"

- "A lot my tastes aren't pleasant. Like bluegrass music always tastes like baking soda."

- "I have taste/shape and some sound/color."

- "I feel as though I experience it at some points during the day."

- "Either it's synesthesia, or a result of my dance training and creativity, but I see choreographies when I listen to music. Not all genres, and not all tracks, though."

- "Numbers and letters/words, music."

- "I do auditory/tactile."

- "I see music."

- "I see numbers, letters, days of the week and some other words in colors."

- "I have links between touch and taste."

- "I see faces or shapes of living things in almost everything."

- "Each letter of the alphabet is a color and I see music as colors moving around."

- "It's subtle and I only become aware of it rarely. But, like, once I was studying biology and there's the lymphocytes number 4 and number 8, and I could not for the life of me have them colored any other way than red for 4 and purple for 8, it was just the right colors of the numbers. I have beautiful and annoying numbers, and my phone number is a pleasant sequence. But it's nothing that stands out too much to me, I don't even think much about numbers."

- "I don't like mine because I can taste words, texture and everything."

- "My autistic daughter sees a different color for each musical note."

- "I "see" words and sounds, like a subconscious ticker-tape. I also taste smells, and feel some sounds. Unpleasant sounds reverberate in my teeth, and pleasant sounds cause a kind of vibration in my head and/or arms."

- "I think mushrooms taste blue, like a periwinkle color. I also sometimes see music in my mind. It looks like a bunch of moving bubbles, strings and spikes of different colors. And I'm pretty sure the letter 'A' is yellow."

- "Sensations and flavors are colors."

- "In many ways I don't even understand it lol but it's fun and trippy lol."

- "I have word/scent/color lap over, since I was a little kid."

- "I can taste numbers."

- "I associate numbers with colors. I don't literally see colors though; I perceive the colors in my mind's eye."

- "I thought something was seriously wrong with me for experiencing this. So much in fact that I never discussed it with a doc or therapist because I was afraid they'd label me schizophrenic or something."

- "I have always associated letters, words and numbers with colors. I thought everyone did until I learned about synesthesia."

- "Letters and numbers trigger an associated color in my mind. 'A' has been yellow for as long as I can remember."

- "All numbers have a specific color, and all the days of the week."

- "Music, numbers, letters, words, calendars, weeks, months, etc."

- "I like your name - first name is sky-blue and last is cherry-red. Great combination! Vowels make them more vivid. Sky-blue - red with certain shade of orange :) That is my first impression but every letter gives special shade. First name has also yellow and a little blue, middle is bluish with light grey-brownish at the end and last one goes through red and yellow to purple and light blue at the end. When I am bored I tend to give names to sunsets and by colors I see on the sky."

- "Sounds have color, colors have taste, and almost everything in my other senses have a tactile experience. Even concepts have a strong tactile sense."

- "Numbers and words have colour to me (like, both the number 4 and the word "mathematics" are red to me, they just are). I used to make coloured calendars according to this."

- "At night I see sounds!
If there's a sudden sound I see a flash of lighting
High pitch it's more like sheet lightning
Constant sound I see a circle like one of them electric domes that give off static lamps Blue and silver
I see the sound of the wind as a white snow storm
It's only in the dark
Sometimes the flash wakes me more then the sound
Something went crash last week I just saw the flash
That woke me up."

- "I see words when people talk and colors when people feel. Different words are different colors and internal typos are highlighted and corrected."

•

Synesthesia can also lead to obsession with colors. Mixed with the love for harmony and routine, it can branch out into color-coding.

- "I color-code:
- the clips I use to close food packaging
- my key holders
- my red tape files
- the tasks on my iCalendar"

- "My classes and homework in my planner.
All the appointments in my work calendar"

- "My order goes:
1 blue
2 teal
3 green
4 olive
5 yellow
6 orange
7 red
8 pink
9 purple
10 lavender
Days of the week start on Monday with blue and skip number 2 and 4 to end with Sundays as purple. I wear

those colors on those days. And organize all of my things in this order.

Parts of the day also have colors (follows the same pattern, but I skip some of the colors).

I homeschool and the subjects are these colors with an additional gray for practical life. Blue and Teal are both different parts of math. Green and Olive are both different parts of language, plus more.

And I chose the basis of this color scheme when I was very very young. Blue comes first because I had the least amount of blue duplos. And everyone knows that the first part of a fun playtime is sorting your toys and assessing the volume of each color."

- "Every spreadsheet I make has columns in rainbow order."

- "I don't color-code anything -- I've tried it but it makes me feel confused."

- "Honestly I just buy things in specific colors. I won't buy/use stuff if it's too weird of a color."

- "I only have stuff like the house, car, clothes, furniture in certain colors like from the blue or green family and black and white. I hate reds."

- "Kids' things. Anything that they each have, like toothbrushes, flashlights, pool towels...for any and all of these things, I always buy red, blue, yellow and each of these corresponds with a particular kid so they don't argue over whose is whose. And I do my file folders: green for financials, blue for info, yellow for personal.

Oh yeah, we also do notebooks (kids are homeschooling): green = science, red = math, yellow = writing, blue = history."

- "I've got synesthesia, so color coding can get er, complicated... The colors have to be "right", otherwise it bothers me a lot. Needless to say, I wear black all the time."

- "My house! Green rooms are for eating and relaxing. Green symbolises life, regeneration and energy to me.
Cooking and laundry room is blue which is my be creative color.
Bathrooms are white to symbolise awake/day
No idea why 🗿 All makes sense to me though 😄"

•

Synesthesia is just one of the wonders we get to experience as autistics. For me it's a constant source of self-entertainment!

If I was offered a pill that magically changed my wiring from autistic to allistic, I would never take it. Ever.
Despite the hardship stemming from being different and trying to get by in a society not made by and for us.

# The End of Wondering

## (or the journey through a maze
## of question marks)

For years on end, questions pouring in, interrogations, minds gone puzzled, by a different attitude, often described as confusing, even disturbing.

Why does this child isolate himself so often?

Why does he speak very little although he shows a rich vocabulary?

Why doesn't he use the first person to speak about himself?

Why does he only draw roads on white sheets?

Why is he so selective with his food? Why does he refuse to take meat and certain vegetables?

Why does he have trouble interacting with his classmates?

"Because he is a trained monkey," thought one lady.

"Because he's awful!", said another.

"Because he is probably gifted," said a third.

But, was it just a "gifted" condition? Admittedly, at the time, this word was very popular, but was not the source of the problem in itself.

And this meager clue was not enough.

And the questions resumed.

Why is he so "different"? Is this really a reason to be constantly mocked by classmates, or even later to be assaulted and robbed?

"It's human nature, what can I say..." some would comment. "There is nothing we can do, there are the strong and the weak and it's always been that way, who would it bother?"

And you, "normal" people, answer honestly: what is most disturbing? This "different" individual who asked nothing of anyone? Or your preformatted, defeatist attitude, ignorant of the real issue?

Why did this now adolescent child completely lose his taste for work after entering high school?

Could it be because of the house move that turned his life upside down? Of the school system which was frankly not adapted to his faculties? Maybe both?

"Good heavens no!", exclaimed the ancestors. "It's in his head, it's all drama! Quick, quick, a psychiatrist and presto, it will get better with medication!"

And so began the guilt trip.

'Why are they bringing me to a psychiatrist?'

'Why do they think I am "mad", "insane", a "born crazy"?'

But nothing helped. And the questions continued ...

Why does he refuse to take these drugs?

Why does he invent a side effect to these drugs?

Why does he not understand that if you are given a treatment for life, you must take it?

The ancestors multiplied the unanswered questions. Without ever being able to find THE right question.

And him? Lost in his guilt, his difference, and his paths, this child who is more or less not asked for his opinion, was plagued by doubt about his own identity. Should he really fit into the mold of "the virile and strong man"? Why this sudden attraction for a feminine side which he could not restrain? Is it due to his difference too?

In fact, the ancestors were far from suspecting that their eldest child was a son, but not only. And he, he who was very aware of their wrath caused by his psychological difference, had taken care to conceal any indication relating to any kind of gender "deviance".

He had just reached the legal age, and in the meantime, other questions arose.

Why does he never drink alcohol?

Why is he never interested in anything related to sex and eroticism?

Two questions for which "because it is his right" was apparently not the right answer.

And with legal age came the first setbacks with the student world and the world of work.

Not authoritarian enough to be a college supervisor, not persuasive enough to be a telemarketer. "And why so?", wondered the employers.

Why? They were obviously not going to seek answers. In the world of work, the numbers prevail, not the social concerns.

And meanwhile, he tried non-stop to develop contacts, at the same time as he tried to unravel the mysteries of this feminine side which seemed strange to him. He wanted to become someone "normal" in the eyes of others, someone who knew how to be social towards others, someone who was neither shy nor withdrawn.

But even there, his presence was not always winning unanimous support.

"He's uneasy!" said some people.

"He's a pervert!" added others, when they learned of his belonging to the transgender community.

A revelation that the ancestors have still not assimilated to this day.

Why is he always trying to disguise himself?

Why does he playact so much when he talks?

Unfortunately, it was not playacting. Oppressed by so many questions and guilt on the part of his peers, the individual suffered more and more, so much so that he began to be anxious when he wanted to open up to others. And even more when he chose to go under the opposite gender. A part of his identity which over the years seemed to him to be part of himself.

Was it due to his innate "difference"?

Luckily, our individual knew a few caring people he/she could count on, who knew better than anyone else what he/she was. But the lack of answer to these questions, coupled with the permanent oppression of a totally incomprehensible society, weighed more and more. And more than once the desire to end it quickly had crossed his mind ...

But then...

A trip to the capital city made him aware of who he/she was. A young woman he/she had known for a long time gave him the opportunity to come and visit her, after

185

six years spent without an opportunity to meet outside social media. She was autistic. He/she was still quite intrigued by this fact, given the reducing vision of autism as instilled by the media the past decades. But he/she couldn't help but feel compassion for people with autism. Her friend was no exception. And there, as the two comrades rejoiced in seeing each other again, THE question arose in his mind. A question that had never reached him before.

"What if I too am autistic?"

That would explain many things. The special interest in roads, anxiety attacks, restrictive eating habits, shyness, isolation, social difficulties ... And after three days and three nights spent in this lost paradise, he/she decided to shoot things clear.

"Yet you don't look autistic." said the young woman.

A little too hasty a judgment, given that the two had not seen each other for six long years. He/she did not want to contradict her, however, for fear of losing a re-acquired friendship after too long.

'But, if I tell my parents, will they still think that I am a drama queen? That I playact, just to attract attention? '

To hell with the ancestors! After all, what could they do about it?

"Be careful though, don't hang on to this too much until it's confirmed," said her close friends. "If it's not autism, aren't you going to take it badly?"

It was a perfectly justified concern.

"What if it really was?" said another close friend, herself diagnosed for some time. "Anyway, you can't know without consulting!"

She was right. He needed an answer as soon as possible.

And thread by needle, from consultation to consultation, the path seemed clearer to him.

"It's probably autism," said a psychiatrist.

"There is an autistic thread present," said another.

And at these words, the friendly words were much more encouraging.

"I can't wait until the diagnosis is made, and I hope for you that it is positive," said his close friends.

And later, in January and February 2020, he/she took the step forward to end his questioning once and for all.

Long sessions, a real ordeal for his mind, with the hope of finally having an answer, after so many years.

Finally, on this day of quarantine, March 27, 2020, the answer finally reached him.

"ASD diagnosis retained."

It's official.

Black on white.

But one question still remains.

"Why couldn't I find out earlier?"
Was it because knowledge of autism was not as advanced before 2000, when he/she had shown his first signs of "weirdness"?

It was not important. The most important was to have found an answer. To be able to explain to the "normal" people why he/she was the way he/she was, and why he/she could do nothing about it.

...

I am autistic.

And this is my story.

May it one day help other autistic people so that they never have to stay too long in a maze of question marks.

•

[Written by Jaeger Elinciel
*www.facebook.com/ShapeShifterJE]*

# The Island and the Bridge

I was born alone on an island.

I can see the mainland quite far away, and I can see many people on it. It is very noisy and very fast there, while on my island, you feel warm and safe.

I started building my bridge a long time ago which allows me to connect my island to the mainland. It is now finished despite the storms that have almost destroyed it several times. But I got there, and it was no accident. I had the help, the energy, and the patience to build it. I am tired but it was essential for me to finish it and I am happy to have achieved it.

Now I have to follow it regularly. Crossing the sea is very tiring too. Not only must we cross with the headwind, but we must also repair this bridge, which crumbles regularly. Once arrived on dry land I find myself in this general agitation that I saw from afar. I'm happy to interact because this is what I wanted. It is both intoxicating and exhausting. I must already be thinking about the way back because my energy is declining at breakneck speed.

I go home to rest, and on the way back, I see other comrades from the surrounding islands.
Some, like me, come back from the mainland and take their bridge. Each island is more or less far from the mainland, and it shows that the bridges are not all built with the same materials and the same solidity.

Some are still in the process of building their bridge, with help from relatives.

Some tried to build their bridge but abandoned it. Their island is too far from the mainland, or they did not have the help, the energy, or even the will to complete it. I don't know why their bridge wasn't made and nobody can explain it except them.

Each person has their story. And just because some people manage to travel on dry land does not mean that they will be able to move there one day.

Their experience of building their bridge could be particularly useful for others, provided that this bridge is respected for what it is: the construction and the preoccupation of an autistic who wants to fight and interact with them.

•

[Written by Grégory Saunier
*The White Rabbit Spoon*
*www.facebook.com/WhiteRabbitSpoon*]

« This message is so simple,
yet it gets forgotten:
The people living with the condition
*are* the experts. »

- Michael J. Fox

## Thank You

Erin Banks
Ginevra
Tina Gheorgudí
Caitlin M.
Susan M.
Kim P.
Nathalie R.
Michel S.
Kayla-Rose Kirkland
Grégory Saunier
Jaeger Elinciel
Lilith Allenspach
Emily Child
Kelebek
Lucinda Y.
Hanna R.
Tamara A.
Dominique

..... for going down the path of often-painful memories and for sharing your intimacy. Thank you for your trust.

Kylie Gray for your creative contribution to the title of this book.

My family, for embracing with genuine interest my quirks and endeavors, and for your unconditional love and support.

The "Aspergers & Autism Safe Room: A Safe Haven For Women On The Spectrum" Facebook Group, for being my mothership. Joining you after I just had my own "OMG I am sure I am autistic, it would explain so much, my whole life, my quirkiness, my struggles, my talents, my behavior, everything!"- Aha-moment helped me validate and process it. It still does.

The Neurodiversity movement, activists, associations and all the autistics who spend some of or all their energy to shift the paradigm about autism and defend the autistic rights.

•

Should you wish to contact the author
or any of the contributors who shared their story,

write to:
anne.cosse@gmail.com

•

Please respect the work of the author and the privacy
of the contributors. They gave their consent for their
story to be published in this book only.

# Table of Contents

Copyright © Anne Cossé, 2020
All rights reserved.
First edition: June 2020
ISBN : 979-10-92669-16-9


Cover design: Rocío Martín Osuna

Printed in Great Britain
by Amazon

24400036R00118